D0761821

The
HOCKEY SCRIBBLER

The

HOCKEY SCRIBBLER

———

GEORGE BOWERING

Published by ECW Press
665 Gerrard Street East
Toronto, Ontario, Canada, M4M 1Y2
416-694-3348 / info@ecwpress.com

MIX
Paper from
responsible sources

FSC
www.fsc.org
FSC® C016245

Al Purdy's poem "Hockey Players" has been
reprinted with permission.
"Hockey Players" by Al Purdy, *Beyond
Remembering: The Collected Poems of Al
Purdy*, edited by Sam Solecki, 2000, Harbour
Publishing, harbourpublishing.com

Cover design: Tania Craan
Author photo: Thea Bowering

To the best of his abilities, the author has
related experiences, places, people, and
organizations from his memories of them.

LIBRARY AND ARCHIVES CANADA
CATALOGUING IN PUBLICATION

Bowering, George, 1935–, author
Hockey scribbler / George Bowering.

Issued in print and electronic formats.
ISBN 978-1-77041-289-7
ALSO ISSUED AS: 978-1-77090-854-3 (PDF)
978-1-77090-855-0 (EPUB)

1. Hockey—Canada. 2. Bowering,
George, 1935–. 3. Authors, Canadian
(English)—20th century—Biography.

1. Title.

GV848.4.C3B673 2016   796.9620971
C2015-907293-X   C2015-907294-8

The publication of *The Hockey Scribbler* has been generously supported by the Canada Council
for the Arts, which last year invested $153 million to bring the arts to Canadians throughout the
country, and by the Government of Canada through the Canada Book Fund. *Nous remercions
le Conseil des arts du Canada de son soutien. L'an dernier, le Conseil a investi 153 millions de dollars
pour mettre de l'art dans la vie des Canadiennes et des Canadiens de tout le pays. Ce livre est financé
en partie par le gouvernement du Canada.* We also acknowledge the Ontario Arts Council (OAC),
an agency of the Government of Ontario, which last year funded 1,709 individual artists and
1,078 organizations in 204 communities across Ontario, for a total of $52.1 million, and the
contribution of the Government of Ontario through the Ontario Book Publishing Tax Credit
and the Ontario Media Development Corporation.

Ontario
Ontario Media Development
Corporation

ONTARIO ARTS COUNCIL
CONSEIL DES ARTS DE L'ONTARIO
an Ontario government agency
un organisme du gouvernement de l'Ontario

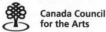

Canada Council
for the Arts

Conseil des Arts
du Canada

Canadä

PRINTED AND BOUND IN CANADA   PRINTING: FRIESENS   5   4   3   2   1

In skating over thin ice our safety is our speed.

−RALPH WALDO EMERSON

This book is for Ewart H. Bowering,
a Canadiens fan who let me have his old skates.

FOLLOWING HOCKEY
in the DESERT

Up Fairview Road running southwest from downtown Oliver, British Columbia, till you got to where the mining town of Fairview used to be, then a right turn off the road into a miniature valley between hillocks, I guess you'd call them, is where you would find a small irregular pond with some bends and narrow spots, and sagebrush islands or sumac bushes growing up from the middle. If it was one of those winters with snow and ice, that's where you would find a shallow frozen pond with snow on top of the ice, and wind tucking drifts of snow against those brittle bushes. This is where kids whose families had moved from the prairies to the South Okanagan would hike to play hockey.

They would get up very early on a Saturday, the way kids will do, and hike up there with shovels and skates and sticks. It would take them till early in the afternoon to get all the new snow off the ice, and then they would drop shovels, pick up sticks and play pond hockey for two hours. Then they would trade skates for boots and get a good downhill start because it would be dark by four o'clock.

These were kids who used to skate in their own back yards in Saskatchewan. They had Russian names and German names and seemingly boundless energy. After church on Sunday they would be back up at the pond, and if it hadn't snowed overnight, they had a whole afternoon of skating hard before going home and doing their chores in the dark.

These kids were really good. They had been playing hockey since getting their first second-hand skates around age four. They would use a bush as a third defenceman. They did not have all that Canadian Tire equipment you see city kids with now, the lightweight goal net and all that. They had taped-up wooden sticks with which they zoomed in on a goal that was simply made of a few jackets with space between them. Any puck that got by the goaltender had to be less than four feet in the air.

I never played with these guys. Taking on a kid from Saskatchewan at hockey would be like trying to out-swim a seal. But I did help with the snow, and I did mark down the goals and assists in a Hilroy. I would have kept time, but really, there was no time up there.

One of those Saskatchewan kids was Tom Moojalsky. He and his brother Sam and sister Marjorie and the youngest kid, who went by the name Baby, used to live at Veregin, outside Kamsack, Saskatchewan, two towns best known as the site of several poems by John Newlove.

Newlove, too, moved from eastern Saskatchewan to British Columbia, and prairie roads and rivers haunted his poems. He was a rainy window intellectual, but he was also a hockey fan. He often threatened to shoot or stab anyone who got between him and the television screen when *Hockey Night in Canada* was on.

I don't remember any hockey poems by John Newlove, though he did not shy away from violence of other sorts. And even his saddest poems about the prairie are immaculately beautiful, such as this little one called "Return Train":

> *A low, empty-*
> *looking, unpainted house;*
> *back of it, the corn*
> *blighted, the tractor*
> *abandoned.*

That's from a 1986 book called *The Night the Dog Smiled*.

The Moojalsky family arrived in town when I was in elementary school. In grade five we all had to make a presentation in front of the whole class. I can't remember what mine was about, but I do remember that Tom Moojalsky explained the rules of ice hockey. He really knew his stuff, too. Remember, this was in a small Canadian town a long way from the nearest hockey rink. So I don't know how interesting this was for the girls in the class, Sylvia MacIntosh, for example, or Joan Roberts, but I don't think that I was the only boy that learned something the day Tom Moojalsky told us what the blue line was for, and what an offside looked like.

I mean we all heard these words on the radio on Saturday nights, but when Foster Hewitt mentioned that Gaye Stewart had fired a shot from the point, I for one did not know what the point looked like.

Of course in that room in the two-storey schoolhouse at the foot of a brown mountain there were other pupils who had lived on farms on the prairie, and they knew what a hockey rink looked like. Kids such as I had seen lots of black-and-white photographs of hockey games. But we did not know what the ice smelled like, or what bodychecking sounded like. I think I remember that Tom gave that presentation again in grade six. Why not? That's how you learn things.

If I remember correctly all these years later, Tom and Sam Moojalsky were two of the boys skating around sagebrush up that hill in the disappearing light. I wish that I could have seen them on the sheet of ice that Tom described in his presentation.

AFFILIATED
with SYL APPS

Living as we did 15 miles from the United States and a long way from Ontario, we did not have many things in our quotidian lives to keep us Canadian. Two things did that: the *Star Weekly* and Imperial Oil's *Hockey Night in Canada*. The *Star Weekly* was apparently a weekend paper back in the shroud that was Toronto, but we got it by mail on the next Thursday. It seemed to be a staple of just about every household, though I do remember that some immigrants from the prairies got a similar weekly from Winnipeg. The comics section had "The Phantom," otherwise unavailable to an Okanagan boy.

The *Star Weekly* came in sections. There was a rotogravure that often had pictures of Easter in Toronto or Christmas in Toronto or Halloween in Toronto. I always snaffled the Phantomless coloured comics section, and during the week my father would read the condensed novel, which was often the most recent Erle Stanley Gardner case. I don't remember my mother's choice or my sister's. I would not read the condensed novel, because I had already decided that you shouldn't read condensed things. I got that idea from the assurance in drugstore paperback westerns that the Pocket Book or Bantam Book in your hand was "complete and unexpurgated."

Hockey Night in Canada was the reason that there was no vehicular or foot traffic along the roads around Oliver (or Osoyoos, or Okanagan Falls, etc.) on early Saturday evenings during the months between October and April. Thanks to the high radio aerials at Watrous, Saskatchewan, or if the weather was all right, CBC's Trail, B.C., station, we could tune in at six p.m. and hear Foster Hewitt say, "Hello, Canada, and hockey fans in the United States and Newfoundland, there are two minutes remaining in the first period and there is no score between the Boston Bruins and the Toronto Maple Leafs."

No, we never got to listen to the whole first period. They didn't in Toronto, either. Maybe they were worried that Maple Leaf Gardens wouldn't fill up. We did not get to listen to the Montreal Canadiens games, either. These were broadcast on CBC's French network. Maybe once a season the Canadiens would play a Saturday night in Toronto, and the excitement would go up. This was especially true in our house, because my father was, for some inexplicable reason, a Canadiens fan, and I was a true blue Maple Leafs supporter.

Here's how true a Maple Leafs supporter could be in the iceless Okanagan Valley thousands of miles from

Maple Leaf Gardens, where Foster Hewitt described games from his perch "high in the gondola": I was a member of the kids' fan club. I saved my allowance and other income and sent away for their stuff. I had a Leafs pennant, glossy photographs with reproduced signatures of men such as Bill Ezinicki and Vic Lynn, an "adjustable" ring (oh, I wish I still had that), and an impressive certificate that said it or I was "officially affiliated with the Toronto Maple Leafs hockey club." I didn't have a firm hold on that word. When I told my father that I and my stuff were "officially afflicted with the Toronto Maple Leafs hockey club," he laughed and laughed as only a Habs fan can.

I had an itchy blue Maple Leafs sweater, too. I think my mother must have got that from the Eaton's catalogue.

I did wonder a lot about that gondola. I knew that a gondola was one of those boats that guys in striped shirts poled around the wet streets of Venice. That didn't seem right. I settled for a boat-shaped thing hanging from the ceiling of Maple Leaf Gardens, with hockey announcers looking down from their scary vessel.

So it would be some years before I would smell the ice of a hockey rink or hear the sound of blades cutting the ice as a player shifted direction. I could hear the crowd at Maple Leaf Gardens because apparently there was a microphone hanging from that boat in the rafters. Foster Hewitt's voice would rise for a rush by the KLM Line, and the Toronto crowd noise would surge. And if a goal were scored, increasing the lead over the unloved Boston Bruins, the crowd might get so loud that Foster had to bellow his famous line, "He shoots. He scores!"

There was one single voice that we could hear, once a

game. In fact, we would wait for it, waiting for an authen-ticating ritual to come across the airwaves, you might say. Once a game, during a moment when there was no PA announcement, and when the 16,000 Torontonians had quieted down, some leather-lunged fan would shout, "Come onnnnnnnnnnn, Teeder!" This was an encour-agement for Ted (Teeder) Kennedy, the young man who would inherit Syl Apps's job as captain of the Maple Leafs. Years later, when I read the obit for Kennedy, who died at 83, I would find out that this loud and faithful fan was a garage-man named John Arnott. Someone told me that before Teeder, he used to yell, "Come on, Peter!" Pete Langelle? I don't know. Maybe I will explain that when I get to my chapter on Port Colborne, Ontario.

So hockey was an aural experience for me, but I was still all wrapped up in the NHL. Part of the reason may have been because my father was, too. I never saw my dad play hockey as I saw him play so many other sports, and I know that he did not see an NHL game until he was over 60, when I took him to a Montreal Canadiens game at the Pacific Coliseum in Vancouver. The only Major League Baseball game he ever saw was an Expos game against St. Louis in Jarry Park that I took him to, also when he was in his sixties.

We were avid listeners, these two males who grew up in the Okanagan desert. Until Canadiens games were added to *Hockey Night in Canada*, he even listened to the Leafs games. I don't know whether he was cheering for them or against them. I do know that he taught me that you were supposed to have a second-favourite team, and his was the Rangers, so he would have cheered for them to defeat my beloved Leafs.

HOCKEY
in PRINT

I don't know how I managed it, but I got a copy of Foster Hewitt's juvenile fiction *He Shoots, He Scores!*, which came out in 1949, and I read it several times. Like all the other hockey books I got, it had terribly amateur artwork on the cover. Thus, hockey, which had made me a Canadian of sorts, taught me that Canadian books were inferior in design. The writing wasn't all that good, either.

Of course I was reading the hockey news in the *Province* and then the *Vancouver Sun*. It was a more literate age then, so there weren't as many pictures to accompany or replace the reportage, but there were some pictures, so I knew what Bill Ezinicki's hair looked like and I knew that Pete Babando was a left-hand shot. In fact one year I bought a scribbler and got some glue somewhere and started a scrapbook of NHL clippings. The idea was that I would cut out the news accounts of all the games and paste them into my scribbler, thus preserving an entire season for some reason.

Over the next six decades I kept coming across this scribbler, which was definitely not thick enough to handle even a 60-game schedule. So a few days ago I thought to myself, "Hey, white-haired geezer, why don't you get that scribbler and maybe copy a few headlines into this book thing you are writing?" Since that day I have been upstairs, downstairs, in my lady's storage room, and have not found it yet. This is always happening to me. However, if I should happen to locate it by some miracle, I will favour you with a few quotations from the hockey journalism of my boyhood.

Once in a while hockey would show up in the popular Canadian magazines such as *Maclean's* or *New Liberty*, but the latter was more likely to have the royal princesses than Charlie Rayner on the cover. In 1948, I got my first subscription to *Sport* magazine, which, like most of the periodicals we got to see, came from the USA. For that reason it had a lot more football stories than hockey stories in its 100 pages. But the first issue I got in the mail, February 1948, had Boston Bruins goalie Frank Brimsek on the cover, and the background was bright yellow, my favourite colour. (I still have this magazine, too.) Of course, I was a little completist kid, so I began looking for issues that preceded my subscription. Don Redmond, the United Church minister's son, was a little older than I, and happily sold me his 1947 issues when I could raise a quarter. I sometimes acquired a second copy so that I could put full-page colour photos of athletes all around my bedroom walls.

But *Sport* would rarely have a hockey player on the cover, especially if he was not a USAmerican, as Brimsek was. If you wanted a magazine with hockey in it, you had to wait for a couple of Canadian mags—*Blueline* and *Hockey Pictorial*. *Blueline*'s first issue was dated October 1954, and *Hockey Pictorial*'s first issue was dated October 1955. That means that both magazines started when I was a teenager in the air force, and I added them to all the baseball magazines I had started collecting when I was 11.

Blueline and *Hockey Pictorial* were even less professional in their design and writing than other Canadian magazines of the time. I was a little embarrassed by this fact, but I saved every issue just the same. In fact I kept them until the summer of 2013, when my wife Jean finally persuaded me to sell them cheap to a dealer, in order to clear some space in the basement storage room. I hated to see them go. Maybe that's why one issue of *Hockey Pictorial* showed up while I was looking everywhere for that scribbler of hockey clippings.

Oh oh, I just had a look at it. It is a little crooked because of being jammed behind a copy of the October 1951 *Hit Parader*. It is all in black and white, except for the touches of red and pink (!) on the cover. The main guy on the cover is Jean Béliveau, "Greatest in Years," but there are smaller pictures of Bill Quackenbush (who was always valuable to me when I was playing an NHL alphabet game in my head), Ted Kennedy, Dick Irvin and Terry Sawchuk. It sold for 25 cents and boasted 34 pages. I bought it in Portage la Prairie. If anyone wants it, I'll let it go for 50 bucks.

Okay, I have to admit that though it was not a great magazine, *Hockey Pictorial* is kind of special to me. It was there that I published my first poem to appear in a national magazine. In April 1957, they printed a letter from me, which I wish that I could reprint for you, but as you know, Jean made me get rid of that mag. However, my career was properly launched in the November 1958 issue, when above an advertisement for Player's cigarettes appeared a 26-quatrain poem entitled "The ABC's of the NHL." It went:

A *is for Armstrong*
George, the Big Chief
Obviously
A most valuable Leaf

B *is for Boom-Boom*
Big noise at the Forum
If the Habs need six goals
Bernie will score 'em

C *is for Cullen*
Brian and Barry
To distinguish between
Is not necessary

D *is for Dickie*
Remarkable Duff
A young future all-star
This kid has the stuff

E *is for Evans*
Who looks pretty nice
Except when you have to
Look up from the ice

F *is for Flaman*
And Fernie and fighter
One of the reasons
The Bruins are brighter

G *is for Godfrey*
A blue line bruiser
Built on the lines
Of a heavy cruiser

H *is for Howe*
Need we say more?
His efforts so often
Determine the score

I *is for Irvin*
A man we remember
Whose teams would be twenty
Games up in December

J *is for Johnson*
The Habs' unknown man
He holds them together
If anyone can

K *is for Kelly*
A wizard on skates
Who keeps Red Wing boosters
Revolving the gates

L *is for Lindsay*
A man of no mystery
His scoring has made him
Left-winger of history

M *is for Moore*
A high-scoring rage
Whose fabulous shot
Stuffs the puck in the cage

N *is for Norris*
A recognized name
The clan owns
50% of the game

O *is for Olmstead*
Who set up the line
That poured all the rubber
Right into the twine

P *is for Plante*
The wandering man
Who comes up with antics
Nobody else can

Q *is for quality*
This overall
Is the thing you will notice
Of classy Glenn Hall

R *is for Rocket*
A fast-moving missile
The Habs now have two
Who will make your hair bristle

S *is for Sawchuk*
The man in a crouch
Which never can be
Misconstrued as a slouch

T *is for Topper*
Boston's durable vet
A good man to have
In front of the net

U *is for Ullman*
A maker of plays
But scoring would win him
A lot more of praise

V *is for Vasko*
A mountainous guy*
You'll never get through him
And seldom get by

W*'s for Watson*
A coach full of fire
Who's pushing the Blueshirts
Higher and higher

---

* At 6-foot-2 and two hundred pounds, Elmer "Moose" Vasko was
considered a giant in the NHL of the fifties.

X *is for danger*
The dramatists say
(A tip) stay out of
Jean Béliveau's way

Y *is for youth*
Which the Leafs have got
And time will tell
If the team can get hot

Z *is for zing*
And zoom as well,
Those words sum up
Today's NHL

You might say that my first nationally published poem was a piece of doggerel, and you would be right. I was writing a lot of doggerel in those days. To make matters worse, this lamentable example was to be followed by a travesty entitled "The ABCs of the NHL past" in the February 1959 issue. You can bet that the letter Q was seldom given better employment than it was here, because Bill Quackenbush was my favourite name from the forties. Both pieces were written while I was still in the air force a couple of years earlier. I do remember that I also wrote a baseball version, and it was, thank the ghost of Granny Hamner, rejected by *Baseball Magazine,* which had printed a letter I had written when I was 17.

A FEW RINKS

It was also while I was in the air force that I got to see my first professional hockey game. This contest took place at Winnipeg's brand new 9,500-seat arena next to the Polo Park Racetrack. When it opened for the 1955–56 season, it was the finest ice rink in western North America, and the biggest deal since the Colisée de Québec was built so that young Jean Béliveau would stay and play for the Québec Aces rather than go openly professional up the river in Montreal.

The Winnipeg Arena was home to the Winnipeg Warriors of the Western Hockey League. The Warriors were an expansion team that year, along with the Brandon Regals. The WHL had started in 1952–53, as a kind of amalgamation of what was left of the Pacific Coast League and the Western Canada League. In 1955–56

Winnipeg's opposition consisted of teams from Seattle, Vancouver, Calgary, Edmonton, Saskatoon, Brandon, New Westminster and Victoria. The league would lose some teams and gain others until 1974 when NHL expansion and the creation of the World Hockey Association would put an end to it. Some of the teams would move to the Central Hockey League. Others would bequeath their rinks to NHL and WHA teams.

In 1955–56, I entered my second winter as a photographer at RCAF Station Macdonald, just south of Lake Manitoba, northwest of Portage la Prairie. Sometimes a carload of us airmen would drive to Winnipeg for the weekend to see a football game or drink beer at one of the breweries' dance halls. On one of these trips a batch of us snuck a mickey of booze each under our warm jackets and attended a game in the beautiful new arena. I do not remember which team the Warriors beat that night, but I like to think it was the Seattle Americans.

I do remember what a rush it was to be at an actual professional hockey arena after all my years of looking at pictures and reading magazine stories. There was the bright light overhead, the echoing bang as a warm-up puck smacked the boards, the steel blades cutting ice, the organist practising his or her cavernous riffs.

But for me the most exciting thing about that night was getting to lay eyes on Bill Mosienko. Bill Mosienko was very famous, and I had heard Foster Hewitt say his name often. I had his stats in my head. It was a lovely (though I would never at that time have used that adjective) story, Bill Mosienko coming to Winnipeg to play professional minor league hockey.

Mosienko was 34 years old. He had just played 14 years for the Chicago Black Hawks. Well, you could really make that 12 years. In his rookie year in the NHL he played in 11 games and got 14 points. Called up from the Kansas City Americans, he scored his first two NHL goals 21 seconds apart. I was six years old; I didn't know till later. His second season was peculiar. For some reason the U.S. would not allow him into the country. The U.S. had belatedly entered the war against Hitler, and I guess Mosienko's name was suspiciously European. Anyway, he played for the Quebec Aces in 1942–43, except for two games in which he played for the Chicago Black Hawks in Toronto. He scored two goals in those two games.

Of course, if you know anything about hockey, you know that Bill Mosienko still owns a record he set in 1952, when he scored a hat trick against the New York Rangers in his favourite duration of 21 seconds. I have no idea what my fellow airmen knew about the NHL, or whether they were tickled to be in the same building as the little guy who, at the time of leaving the NHL, was the seventh all-time with 540 points. But here's what I was looking for: a leader, a captain, a *creator* of that damned team, a pretty old guy who could have played another few years in Chicago, but who was here giving professional hockey to the town he grew up in.

He grew up a scrawny kid with Ukrainian-speaking parents in the north end of Winnipeg, and when he was playing in Chicago on a line with two Bentleys, he was about 5-foot-7 when he took his skates off, and weighed 160 pounds on a heavy day. So just the way it happened when he was a kid, the bigger players' strategy was to bash him around. Despite that, he won the Lady Byng Trophy in 1945, scoring 54 points and serving exactly zero minutes in penalties.

That's why I liked him.

In his first year with the Winnipeg Warriors he got two minor penalties, but he also scored 64 points. He led his team to the league championship, and then carried them to victory over Quebec to give his home town the Edinburgh Trophy, which went to the best minor league professional hockey team in Canada.

I don't remember how many points Bill Mosienko got the night I saw him play and I don't remember how cold it was that night in Winterpeg. But I saw the smallest guy skating away from his pursuers in the biggest ice rink I had ever seen.

As I said, the Winnipeg Warriors were the first professional hockey team I ever saw live. But my being in the air force had helped me to attend some Ontario Junior hockey games in the fall of 1954. After doing my basic training at Saint-Jean-sur-Richelieu, Quebec, over the summer, I went to RCAF Borden, Ontario, for training as an aerial photographer. The closest city to Borden was Barrie, where I sat out Hurricane Hazel, and where I had a girlfriend named Jean, who had red hair and played defence for the General Electric women's hockey team, but almost as importantly, where I saw a few home games of the Barrie Flyers of the Ontario Hockey Association.

I had never seen junior hockey, so I was unprepared for the violence perpetrated by those guys who were about my age. Those unhelmeted lads smashed each other with sticks, or dropped sticks and smashed each other with fists. I got the impression that they were enacting what they thought being a young male was all about. The game on the ice in the Barrie Arena didn't resemble the game I watched in my head while listening to Foster Hewitt.

The outfits these OHA youths wore were somewhat worse for wear, with what looked like moth holes in their socks and visible stitching on their shorts. No one, by the way, could explain why ice hockey players wear long stockings and shorts held up by suspenders. But there I was, a boy/man who was interested in sports and planned to be interested forever. It plain excited me to see the Flyers take on the Guelph Biltmores and the Galt Terriers. The Flyers had beaten the St. Boniface Canadiens for the Memorial Cup two seasons back. They wore yellow and black because they were affiliated with the Boston Bruins.

The Flyers would have a losing season in 1954–55, and when I look at their roster for that season I don't see any NHL stars. But I do remember the Cullen brothers. They played for the St. Catharines Teepees, who had won the most recent Memorial Cup. In my memory both Brian Cullen and Barry Cullen were out there smashing and bashing the Flyers, but according to the rosters I have seen, Brian had already gone to play in Pittsburgh. However, I was duly impressed by the Cullen I saw, who was the second-highest scorer for the Teepees, and who knew how to cause blood to appear on an opponent's forehead.

I remember that I did not much care for the mayhem, but I was excited to hear skates on the ice, and feel the chill under my jacket.

The air force helped me get into other arenas, too. In the springs of 1956 and 1957, I was on temporary duty at RCAF

Namao, just north of Edmonton. The RAF, the USAF and the RCAF were working out of RCAF Cold Lake, way up north, on a secret high-altitude camera, and I was stuck in a photo lab at Namao, being secret in the dark. Anywhere you wanted to walk at the Namao base, you had to walk on duckboards laid over the mud. Occasionally some of us would hitchhike into Edmonton for a good time. Once a couple of us got a ride in the back of a police cruiser, where we slouched as low as we could get.

I don't remember what we used to do in Edmonton, which was not exactly the entertainment capital of the Western World in 1956. I suppose we went to a beer parlour or two, as any red-blooded youths would do. Maybe we had a hamburger somewhere. I think I kind of remember seeing the Alberta legislature building from the south side of the river, so I must have had my usual experience of terror while crossing the High Level Bridge.

But I do recall being inside the old Edmonton Gardens, a rickety, leaking hulk with hard wooden seats and poor sightlines. It was popularly known as the "Cow Barn" because of its first use as a stock pavilion, but it was now the hockey home of the Edmonton Flyers, a Detroit farm team in the Western Hockey League. In the 1955–56 season, the Flyers finished fourth out of five in the Prairie Division of the WHL despite having Gerry Melnyk, Don Poile and Al Arbour on their roster.

Hockey had been long over for the year on April 26, 1956, when we found our seats in the Cow Barn to see two men fight without skates on their feet. This would be the only time I would ever see a world champion boxer in action. The champion was Archie Moore, one of my heroes. He was the light heavyweight champ, but did most of his fighting as a heavyweight. A half-year before, he had knocked Rocky Marciano down in Marciano's last heavyweight title defence.

Here in Edmonton all the talk was about the city's first professional boxing match in years and years. The other boxer was a palooka named Sonny Andrews, who made a career of getting knocked out in Los Angeles by guys like Frankie Daniels and J. D. Reed. Archie Moore had already TKO'd him in Sacramento two years earlier. Okay, Sonny Andrews wasn't much of a threat, but here it was, the first pro bout in Edmonton in most people's memories. It was a non-title match, but these were big American men, eh?

When Archie took off his robe it was easy to see why he did most of his boxing as a heavyweight those days. A good amount of his two hundred and some pounds was hanging outside his big trunks, and as he moved around the ring we would see it jiggling quite a bit.

And he was 39 years old. Many decades later the boxing world would get used to middle-aged thumpers huffing and puffing around the squared circle, but back in the fifties, most fighters retired in their early to mid-30s. Remember this, though: Archie started his boxing career in 1935, but did not become a world champion until he decisioned Joey Maxim, who had TKO'd the great Sugar Ray Robinson. In 1952, at the age of 36, Archie Moore became the light heavyweight champ.

He had always been a very active boxer, having a match nearly every month. I have to admit that after seeing his pictures so often in my magazines, I was a little upset to see the fat on him. This was my first ever pro fight, and the venue had already eliminated some of the glamour.

But I was a fan, and I liked to think that I was going through another significant moment in the drama of my life. I felt superior to most of the crowd around me, especially when they started booing. They were booing because Archie started the bout using his "turtle defence." Now, I was a kid who read, so I knew about the turtle defence, and I came to understand that the crowd in Edmonton was not particularly given to reading, nor to the sweet art of manly defence. Years later the great Muhammad Ali would swipe Archie's strategy and call it the "rope-a-dope."

The turtle defence means that instead of hopping all over the ring looking for an opening, you cover up with your big 10-ounce gloves and your forearms, tucking your head in the way a turtle does, and usually backing into the ropes, where you can tire out your opponent, who is flailing away with both hands, running down his batteries. In Edmonton, Archie's face wasn't visible to Sonny Andrews nor to the crowd. Archie didn't throw punches. He was putting on a terrific display of defensive skill, and the Edmonton mopes who had not had a professional fight in their town for years didn't get it. They booed an overweight legend. I was enjoying seeing an artist who just may have been the best fighter ever, and learning a lot about Alberta.

Finally, Archie got tired of the booing. All right, he must have thought, if they don't want boxing I will just send them home. In the fourth round he came out of his corner and hit Sonny. Then he hit him again. I can't remember how many times he hit him, but pretty soon Archie said okay, there you go, and walked off while

Sonny Andrews lay on the floor and a few thousand Edmontonians thought to themselves, it's over? That's all I get? Less than four rounds?

At least, that was what I hoped they were saying to themselves.

That LITTLE
RED SCRIBBLER

I had a hunch. Maybe I gave up the idea of ever using
that little reddish scribbler, and tossed it in with the manuscripts and letters and such that I send to my archive
at the National Library. After getting my sweetheart to
move some of the boxes in the storage space, and digging
through a couple of those boxes, I did indeed find it. It's
just the way I remembered it, which doesn't happen all
that often. As I opened this little book I glued 64 years
ago, I got all nutsy-crushy. I will explain that. It is a term
invented by me and my best pal Willy, who studied in
Japan in the early sixties, and went on to marry a Japanese
woman, and came to live a life half in Japanese. We often
engage in nostalgia. The Japanese term for a happy-sad
nostalgia is *natsukashii*. Impressed by the similarity of the
Japanese and English words, we coined the third word

"nutsy-crushy," because it seemed in a way to *feel* right. I am happy to say that more and more people we know are using the term.

This is very peculiar. At the moment of typing these words I am sitting in a house on the edge of the sea in a grubby little fishing village named Chicxulub in the Mexican state of Yucatán. Beside me is the little scribbler in which I pasted stories in the fall of 1949. You might think that this is the only connection between this warm coconut spot with its January sunshine, and the kind of ice that comes under hockey. But a few days ago in the main square of the capital city of Mérida, we met a guy wearing not a T-shirt but a red Montreal Canadiens jersey with the number 10 and the name Lafleur on the back. He wasn't sure, but we told him that it was not a football jersey. I will likely remind you of him when it comes time to discuss hockey duds.

The scribbler. It took me a while, but I figured out that the season I was going to memorialize was 1949–50. I started with all the pre-season news as presented by the *Vancouver Sun*, which we got a day late in Oliver, B.C. By the time I had filled it up, using every inch of space, the season was only nine games old. Apparently I never started a second scribbler, maybe because I had started working on the comic-strip game I had invented.

On the inside front cover, along with something about an ordered car part in my mother's handwriting, is a photograph of King Clancy and Maurice Richard, and the printed remark, "What a difference a year makes." They are smiling like crazy, which will make you wonder where the real Rocket Richard is, at least. A year earlier, then-referee Clancy had slapped the Rocket with a $25 fine for "talking to him too freely." Now the coach of the new Cincinnati Mohawks of the American Hockey League, Clancy is smoking a cigarette and wearing a double-breasted suit and a tie. Richard? How many times did you ever see him in a tie?

How would these two hockey brand names do in the season of 1949–50? The Canadiens would finish second and be knocked out of the playoffs in five games by the New York Rangers, but Richard would beat out Gordie Howe for the right-wing position on the All-Star Team, and he would lead the league in goals with 43. Clancy in Cinci? Well, the Mohawks, who had until then been the Washington Lions, wound up with the worst record in the 10-team AHL.

Mohawks? Well, in the Iroquois Confederacy, the Mohawk people were known as "the Keepers of the Eastern Door," defenders of the confederacy against threats from that direction. Cincinnati, situated in the Middle-west, and across the river from Kentucky, was in Shawnee territory. The Mohawk people, who never called themselves that, did not sport that famous haircut, and they did not have any real estate in southern Ohio—and they certainly did not open any gas stations in British Columbia.

You have probably noticed by now that in my kind of hockey book there is a lot going on besides skating and awkward fisticuffs.

Frank Brimsek, who came from a dicky burg in Minnesota, and was pretty big at 5-foot-9, was not a Mohawk, but he became a Black Hawk in 1949. I liked Brimsek, as you have likely picked up, and the first real page of my scribbler has side-by-side pics of him in the traditional pose of a goalie, hands on knees in front of a net. These shots present him as a Bruin and a Hawk, the second taken at North Bay, Ontario, where the Chicago team trained for the season opener, and they remind us of the biggest trade of the off-season. The Bruins traded him for cash and played their season with Jack Gelineau between the pipes.

Brimsek would play all 70 games for the Hawks that season, for a few thousand dollars. In those days NHL players would get summer jobs selling cars or delivering ice. Now 6-foot-5 guys who score three goals a year and can't spell "you're" are making a million dollars a season. Don't get me started.

I spend lots of time these days looking through my little scribbler. One of the big pre-season stories was the saga of Danny Lewicki. Eighteen-year-old Lewicki, already famed for his dipsy-doodle skating, had signed a C-form agreement with the Toronto Maple Leafs. But Danny was from the Lakehead, and he didn't want to play junior hockey for the Toronto Marlboros. Managing director Conn Smythe of the Leafs said, "If Lewicki is not able to play for Marlboro juniors he won't play junior hockey anywhere else."

Remember when sports franchises thought that they "owned" players? Remember when the reserve clause was still operating in the Major League Baseball monopoly, and if you didn't like the way they treated you, you went and got five times the salary in the Mexican League? Remember how the MLB monopoly also owned the U.S. court system and banned Mexican League jumpers from later playing in the U.S.?

Conn Smythe, according to my scribbler, was bragging about the promise his Leafs showed for the 1949–50 season. He was especially high on a forward line he had assembled on the first day of training school in St. Catharines: George Armstrong, Danny Lewicki and Jack McKenzie. But the young dipsy-doodler from up north was not a happy camper. He had signed that C-form, but he refused to write his name on a Maple Leafs contract, because he did not want his Toronto skating to be in a Marlies sweater. So the Canadian Amateur Hockey Association suspended him from "organized hockey." The suits and the press always joined in referring to him as "Blond Danny." Screw you, said the teen from Fort William, and got a job as an apprentice with Canadian National Railways in Stratford. As a kid at the Lakehead he had seen as many trains as he'd seen hockey players.

So it is with no surprise that a few pages later in the scribbler we see a headline that tells us that there are "Only 13 Rooks in NHL This Season" and no Maple Leafs are mentioned. A dozen of those rookies had "stood the gaff in minor league competition." The thirteenth was the aforementioned Jack Gelineau, who had played the last three years as goalie for McGill University and was making the jump to Boston.

The next we see of Danny Lewicki is in a confusing article by Jack Sullivan (Canadian Press staff writer). The article is titled "Eastern Scribes Put Leafs, Wings Atop Hockey Poll." (This was the kind of language I learned to use when I was a teenage sportswriter.) A little bit of the article is about the "scribes'" predictions, and the rest is about the saga of the young Blond. Sullivan reprises the

CNR story and then talks money. This is the part that is not clear: "There must have been many cocked eyebrows when Danny made $10,000 a year for two years, plus a $2,500 bonus as his playing price for the Leafs." I am going to guess that by "made," Mr. Sullivan meant "asked." Apparently that was a heck of a lot to ask in 1949, especially for a blond 18-year-old. They should have gone and looked at the shack he lived in when he was a young Uke in Fort William. He lived with a lot of other people.

Smythe did go on to say that Danny was a heck of a hockey player, and Sullivan calls Smythe "as canny a judge of hockey flesh as the next expert." Here you see the management-press combine's conception of their product as something like government-inspected beef. The canny Smythe may have had a business deal in mind when he praised his rebellious property as "more like Aurel Joliet than anybody I've seen." Anyone in Montreal could have told you what high praise that was. Aurèle Joliat was third in career goals when he retired, and made it into the Hockey Hall of Fame in 1945, two years before Smythe's pronouncement. At 5-foot-9, Lewicki was also bigger than Joliat.

Unfortunately, there is no further mention of Danny Lewicki in my scrapbook. But largely because of the noise made by that little scrapper, the Canadian Parliament put an end to the C-form less than a century after slavery was banned in the United States. Lewicki was one of my heroes then, and he is still one of my heroes, despite some rumours I have heard recently. He was a feisty little guy who grew out of a really grim childhood situation and then got whacked by all the management and league dorks for the rest of his life, mainly because he did not pull his forelock and say "yez, boss," just because he was smaller and poorer. Here's the short version of one incident. In the last game in which the great referee Red Storey officiated, he missed a call that led to a visiting team's goal. It looked as if the home crowd was going to kill him, so Lewicki handed the ref his stick, and Storey used it to save his life and escape the arena. Red Storey got retired, and Danny Lewicki got blackballed. I wish someone would write a book about Danny Lewicki. Actually, someone did. See Danny Lewicki's *From the Coal Docks to the NHL*, Randy Warren Accent Printing & Graphics (2006).

The other ongoing story immortalized in my scribbler was the fracas in Chicago. Apparently some Chicago fans were getting on the visiting Montreal Canadiens, who were in the process of losing an early season game 4–1. Habs defenceman Kenny Reardon, well-known for his ability to bash opposing forwards, was greatly irritated by a steelworker in a portion of the stands that could be reached by a hockey stick. Reardon reached the fellow's scalp, arousing the need for six or 10 stitches, it was later reported. There was, of course, a commotion, during which Billy Reay and Leo Gravelle also swung their instruments outside the playing area.

Reardon and Gravelle got off without penalties, but Reay received a misconduct call. Then the fan (called "Gabich," "Garbich" and "Gerbich" in the papers) sued the Montrealers, and Gravelle and Reardon wound up behind bars in downtown Chicago, a city, you will remember, unfamiliar with violence. The sports reporters pounced.

It was somehow a more innocent time. All this seemed to be some kind of fun as far as hockey people were concerned. My scribbler holds one large photo of Canadiens manager Dick Irvin and Chicago manager Bill Tobin saying tut tut to Reardon and Gravelle, who are on the other side of some good sturdy jailhouse bars. Everyone is wearing the ample suits and overcoats of the post-war era. Next is a photo of the fan, George Grbich (probably), also in a double-breasted suit, with a bandage on his forehead.

The players were released on $200 bonds, so that they could catch a midnight train with the rest of the Canadiens. They were scheduled to attend a hearing back in Chicago on November 14. Meanwhile the sportswriters made jolly good fun of the whole affair. One Toronto "scribe" suggested that his colleagues stop referring to "firing," "drilling" and "shots," and to stop calling hockey sticks "offensive weapons" and the like. The Chicago cops were jittery, he contended, after all the Capone years.

George Grbich didn't see the humour. But "I'm not mad at anyone," he said, though he let the charge of assault stand.

NHL president Clarence Campbell showed the usual deep thought of hockey's administrative types by warning fans to keep off the ice. The fact that blood was flowing in the spectators' area that night in Chicago was supposed to be overlooked. The NHL then floated a story that one fan had jumped out onto the ice to chase a man in a red sweater and skates.

But the "scribes" were not about to let an early season party fade away. One bard started a piece about the weekend's schedule laconically: "National Hockey League teams will wield their deadly weapons on four fronts this weekend. So long as the customers heed league president Clarence Campbell's warning to stay off the ice, the mortality rate on fans should be low. Even if tickets are still at a premium, the players can't afford to alienate too many fans' affections with their Chicago tommy-guns." Then in his next paragraph he lets us know the era's attitude toward on-ice mayhem: "But there are enough issues to settle in the week-end games to guarantee they'll be trying to use their sticks with deadly effect on opposing goalies—and, fair enough, on one another."

Fair enough?

That weekend the Toronto Maple Leafs were to invade the ice at Chicago Stadium. Our jokester in the Toronto press contingent could not let the amusement die: "Incidentally, they say around Chicago that the Hawks may issue a football helmet to fan George Garbich, the 33-year-old steelworker whom Kenny Reardon clipped. There's always the chance that the Leafs may try to overtake Canadiens' prison-bar publicity by teeing off on the patched Garbich scalp."

You will have noticed the reference to a football helmet. The notion of a hockey helmet seems not to have been born yet. On the inside back cover of my scribbler, the last item is a big picture of George Grbich. The second-to-last item is a headshot (pardon the term) of the great Canadiens goalie Bill Durnan. He is sucking on his first post-game cigarette and there is blood on his white jersey. His hair is all wet and tousled and there is a big bloody gash next to his left eye, from which more blood drips down his cheek. The last sentence under the picture goes: "Hockey players have many eye accidents, some have been known to have lost their sight, which is the cause of a controversy amongst hockey 'big guns' as to whether or not goalies should be made to wear a mask over the face."

It was around this time, I am sort of puzzled to remember, that I changed my life's ambition from my being a policeman to being a sportswriter. In my defence, though, I will say that when I wrote to Bob Broeg of the *St. Louis Post-Dispatch* about it, I had in mind being mainly a baseball writer.

As I mentioned, that scribbler was pretty skinny. The last league-standings in it look like this:

Toronto	4	1	3	11
Detroit	5	2	1	11
Montreal	4	4	1	9
Chicago	3	4	2	8
New York	2	4	3	7
Boston	2	5	2	6

At the end of that first 70-game season, the Red Wings were comfortable in first place, and went on to win the Stanley Cup final series 4–3 over the Rangers.

When Reardon and Gravelle appeared before a Chicago judge in November, the latter let them off, ruling that the fans had been the aggressors. Later in the season Reardon announced publicly that he was going to make Cal Gardner take 14 stitches to the mouth. The league made Reardon post a $1,000 bond, and gave him back the money after the season because Reardon had not made good (an odd word, wouldn't we say?) on his threat.

JOE
MAKSE

I have mentioned Tom Moojalsky, my schoolmate who came from snow country on the prairie to live in our desert valley. He now lives in southern Alberta, and I still hear from him via social media. When I was a kid, the South Okanagan was an agricultural area to which lots of people were immigrating from points east. One of these people was Joe Makse, who became one of my best friends. Joe and his family came to Osoyoos from Kirkland Lake in northern Ontario.

There was a big middle-European population in Osoyoos, and sure enough, Joe's parents had come to Canada from Yugoslavia, staying for a while in mining country before getting a little orchard in the Okanagan. After the breakup of the USSR and the coming apart of Yugoslavia, Joe always said that his folks came from

Slovenia. When we were 11, Joe's favourite baseball player was Andy Pafko.

Joe was as much a sports fan as I was, if not more. In later years he taught history in Trail, B.C., and supported the hockey teams there. He also taught and coached Jason Bay, who would become a Major League slugger. He must have had mixed feelings when in 2009, the ex-National Leaguer got 36 home runs and 119 RBIs, his best slugging year ever, for the Boston Red Sox. For this was my friend Joe's only fault: he was a devotee of the New York Yankees. I got Joe to teach me how to curse in Serbo-Croatian so I could curse the Yankees in more than two languages. Joe had the nerve to maintain that Joe DiMaggio was the best hitter even after I told him that that distinction belonged to Ted Williams.

I have to tell you that it was awful during the six high school years that we spent together. The Yankees won five pennants and the Red Sox won nary a one, though in 1948 and 1949 they came second by one game. I did often point out that Ted Williams was always, when he wasn't at war somewhere, either winning batting titles or barely missing them, while no Yankee was getting a sniff at one.

But Joe was from northern Ontario, eh? The lake at Kirkland Lake froze over in late fall, and everyone wore skates suspended from their necks when they weren't actually out on the ice. The Blue Devils had won the Allan Cup in 1940. The July 10, 1969, edition of the *Northern Daily News* would feature a big hockey story under the headline "Kirkland Lake—The Town That Made The NHL Famous" (they were quoting Foster Hewitt) and follow that with "Over 25 Boys From K.L. Have Played

NHL Hockey." Okay, the town was, as I knew from listening to Joe and checking it out in the mags, a cold bed of ice hockey.

Ted Lindsay wasn't born there, but he played junior hockey in Kirkland Lake before skating his way into the Detroit Red Wings organization. He would be the left winger on the best forward line that played during my boyhood. He was, like other players I have mentioned, only 5-foot-8, but he earned the nickname "Terrible Ted." And here is another reason I liked him: just as I liked Danny Lewicki for getting rid of the C-form yoke, I liked Ted Lindsay for working tirelessly to fight the Norris syndicate, which controlled all four of the U.S. NHL franchises, and get his fellow players to agree to form the NHL Players' Association, the first successful players' union in hockey. The owners pulled all kinds of dirty tricks to try to defame Lindsay and hide their own crooked financial practices, but Lindsay was a tough little left winger, and now in the age of enlightenment we have the Ted Lindsay Award, which is conferred *by members of the NHL Players' Association* to the NHL's most outstanding player.

A lot of people would say that in the postwar era, Kirkland Lake was both Ontario's biggest gold-mining burg and ice hockey's biggest resource town. So when my buddy Joe Makse said something about hockey I knew that I was getting the goods.

It was not that I ever saw Joe playing hockey or any other sport. Like me, he was a fan, and a knowledgeable one. Of course, his favourite players were southern Slavs. It was just a tad too early for the Mahovlich brothers, so he settled for anyone who could have been Slovenian, or Croatian, or maybe even Slovakian, like Joe Klukay. Sometimes we would play hockey alphabet. "Sid Abel," I would say. "Butch Bouchard," Joe would return. "Pete Conacher," I would suggest. "Woody Dumart," Joe would say, and do that little dance he did.

"Wait, wait," he once adjured, "I want to change my *B* from Butch Bouchard to Pete Babando!" I tried to explain to him that you don't get to change your *B* or any other letter, and besides, I tried to explain, the point is to get a *B* or a *W* or whatever you were trying to get. The point was not to look for the name that would be the most fun saying. Although, it is a lot more fun, all these years later, to say "Pete (wait for it) BaBANdo!" I remember that even Foster Hewitt, with his overcoat Ontario voice, seemed to like saying it. Especially when, on St. George's Day in 1950, the Red Wings and Rangers went into the second overtime in game seven of the Stanley Cup Finals, and Pete BaBANdo scored the goal that made Detroit the champs.

But Joe and I had had our greatest moment a month earlier, in Room 20 of Southern Okanagan High School in Oliver, B.C. Room 20 was the Study Hall, a room so deep that it formed the little central arm of the big E, which was the shape of our school. Stood for Education, I suppose. Here is what you were supposed to do in the Study Hall: because your timetable had some blanks in it rather than serious stuff like Social Studies and Industrial Arts, you were expected to sit at a desk in Study Hall and do your homework or assigned reading. That didn't work well for me, because I always did my Science homework during French class, my French homework during English class and so on. So I usually spent my time reading a Max

Brand novel or drawing comic strips. Whenever we could work it out, Joe Makse and I would sit beside each other in one of the back, back rows.

The supervisor was often the metalwork teacher, Mr. Raeburn. He had a wheeze, and used it when he spoke, along with some coughing, and he could not pronounce Joe's last name. "Wheeze, cough, Maskee," he would say when calling the roll. He was a lot like the Toronto Maple Leafs coach who could not say "Mahovlich," but always called his future Hall of Famer and senator "Maholovich."

Anyway, Joe and I knew how to pronounce all the hockey players' names, including Ed Kryzanowski and Bep Guidolin (5-foot-8), and during those 40 minutes in study hall on that April day in 1950, plus a half hour the next day during lunch, Joe and I wrote down the names of every player who was playing for the (misnamed) Original Six teams that week. Each team was allowed to dress 16 players plus two goaltenders, so Joe and I had to come up with 108 names. In fact we came up with a few more than that because of injury call-ups and so on. The Toronto Maple Leafs used a total of 25 players over that season, though guys like Andy Barbe and Dusty Blair didn't get much in the way of ice time. I don't even remember anything about them now.

I wish Joe and I had done this in, say, 1947. If we had, I would have insisted that I get to write down the names of Don Metz and Nick Metz. When I was 11 years old, lying on the living room floor in my pyjamas and listening to *Hockey Night in Canada*, I was crazy about the Metz brothers. I had no idea that they were from Saskatchewan or that Gord Drillon was supposed to be the Leafs' savior.

I was just thrilled when I heard Foster say their names. I figured from their names that Nick was the dashing handsome one and that Don was the quiet resourceful younger brother. In Toronto they were third-line players, defensive specialists who would make Turk Broda's life easier. I didn't know all that stuff, not me on the rug in a dinky Okanagan village.

Sure, I could tell you the names of the other Leafs, from Broda to Gaye Stewart to Bob Goldham, but I dreamed of being the third Metz, carrying the puck up centre and passing off to Don, with Nick there for the rebound, eh? And somewhere I had read about the 1942 Stanley Cup Final. The Red Wings had Toronto down three games to none. My guy Don Metz had watched those games while wearing a suit and tie. Desperate times call for desperate actions. Toronto coach Hap Day benched his sniper Drillon, and put a hockey outfit on Don Metz and sent him out there to check the Red Wings forwards into the ice.

But here's what Don did. He checked the Red Wings forwards just enough for a 4–3 win. Then in game five he had three goals and two assists. He had amassed a total of two goals and five assists in the 25 games he had played in the regular season. Then he went out in game 6 and got the winning goal. The Leafs won game seven and became the first team in any sport to come from a 3–0 disadvantage to win a series. They were the last, too, until the Boston Red Sox played a similar trick on the universally detested New York Yankees to win the 2004 American League pennant.

So you can have your Sutter brothers and your Esposito brothers and your *frères* Richard. You can have the whole Hextall clan. I really liked the Mahovlich brothers. In fact

Frank Mahovlich was once my travel agent. But you can have them, too. I will take Nick and Don Metz.

Joe Makse fell off a ladder and died a couple years ago, and he took a lot of my boyhood with him. I wish like crazy that he was still here on the planet. If someone challenged me now to name the players in the NHL, I would have a hard time coming up with enough to put together just one of the 30 teams.

WORLD
CHAMPIONS

Eventually there was hockey in the Okanagan, and according to the sports historians, if that is not too grand a term, it was pretty good hockey. If you were a pretty good hockey player in the early fifties, there were not many professional teams on the continent, and you had to go to Owen Sound or Moncton or Kamloops to sign up with a senior league team. The Okanagan Senior Amateur Hockey League started in 1951, with three teams: the Kamloops Elks, the Vernon Canadians and the Penticton Vees. In the 1952–53 season, the Kelowna Packers joined the league. This was all pretty exciting for people in the Okanagan, including me. I was in my last year of high school in that second season of the OSAHL. I didn't get to many games. You had to get up to Penticton, 27 miles north of Oliver, and then have the money to get into the rink. Still, I did manage to be inside Penticton Memorial Arena a few times during the league's decade of operation.

So I got to smell that peculiar odour of the ice before it gets all scratched up by hockey blades. I got to hear that swish as skates go by and the skater puts on the brakes. I got to hear that echo when the shooter misses the net and the hard puck bangs off the end boards. I admit right now, years after I quit going to professional hockey games, that it was a thrill to be in that rink, to feel that little chill and see the bright blue line before white streaks appeared across it.

I don't remember anything, really, about that Penticton Memorial Arena, but I do remember the time I was sitting there with my dad, a few rows up from the boards, excited as heck to see swooshing figures in green and white skating past the foe. A puck came into the crowd, and my dad nimbly snatched it out of the air. My dad was not a hockey player, not in my memory (though I do recall that he played broomball in the old wooden rink in Greenwood in the forties), but he was a basketball player and a first baseman in baseball. Then what did he do? He tossed the puck back onto the ice before play could resume. That's the kind of guy he was, and that is the way sport was in his day. I thought, "You goof!" And I loved him for doing what he did.

It was kind of odd, having an ice hockey team in the sunny Okanagan. Some winters there was no snow, though some winters saw ice on the lakes, and it must have been really cold in the olden days, because my father told me about someone driving a Model A car halfway across Lake Okanagan from the beach in Peachland. The Penticton Vees got their name from three varieties of peaches picked in the 90 degree Fahrenheit days of August. Penticton's motto was "The City of Peaches and Beaches." The big summer parade happened during the Peach Festival. In August 1948, I stood on the side of Main Street and saw the first Peach Festival parade. The honoured guest sweetheart was Alexis Smith, the Hollywood star who went from Penticton to Hollywood to star with Fred MacMurray in *Dive Bomber.* The sash-costumed queen of the event was called Miss Val Vedette.

Kelowna had its famous regatta. In years to come Osoyoos had its Cherry Festival and Oliver would have its Apricot Funday. But in Penticton they named their parade queen and their hockey team after a soft fuzzy tree-fruit. In 1948, when I was 12, there were three varieties of peach that started with "V". There were the Valiants, the Vedettes, and the oddly spelled (then) Veterens. Curiously, I think, the first Queen Val Vedette, Beverly Anne Young, who was also the best-looking one ever, had that strange title laid on her by her parents. A few years later, the people in charge of selling peaches decided that the three varieties were so much like each other that they might as well just be called Vees.

Well, since the Kelowna team was called the Packers, you can imagine some of the newspaper headlines as the Vees spent most of their first season at the bottom of the standings. In their second year they finished third, but had a great series of playoffs and appeared in the Allan Cup finals against the Kitchener-Waterloo Flying Dutchmen, going down in five games on Ontario ice. In their third season they amazed the country, finishing first in the OSAHL, and then fighting through eight games, including three ties, with the Winnipeg Maroons, before facing the famous Sudbury Wolves in the Allan Cup final. The games were played in three of the OSAHL rinks, and after the first four games the Wolves were up 3–1. At the end of regulation time, game 5 was tied 5–5. Then the gallant sweaty Vees scored to win that game and the next two, to become the champions of Canada.

I was there.

I wasn't in Memorial Arena. There was no chance of snaffling a seat inside. But I was in Penticton that night, a skinny 18-year-old with hardly any money but filled with excitement and worldliness. I got the worldliness over the preceding fall and spring, which I had spent in Victoria, going to college and getting into my first beer parlour. I don't know where I got whatever I was drinking this night, but there was a lot of it being passed around in downtown Penticton. Some of the celebration took place in a big hall with a stage, and on that stage was a small band, and for some reason the drummer took off somewhere, and there I sat, on his stool, playing his drums with a piano guy and a bass guy and I don't remember who else. I had played a little drums during the winter in Victoria, played pretty darn bad, knew how to hold the sticks or brushes but with no technique that was not self-taught. I sincerely hope that I was not up on that stage for long.

Because I was a skinny, non-shaving 18-year-old doctor. You see, either in that same hall or another one, some hockey officials had the famous Allan Cup, and in the cup was some less-than-famous drinkable generally used for low-level celebrations. If it was an effervescent wine, it was the bubbly misgrown in Kelowna. Maybe it was beer.

Maybe it was potato champagne. Whatever it was, there was a long lineup of people waiting to take a glug out of the Allan Cup. Twice I pushed my way to the front of the line, requesting, "Let me through, please. I'm a doctor." I don't know why it worked. Maybe everyone was drunk in a friendly manner. Maybe no one was really eager to drink that stuff. Whatever the case, I wound up with a lot of it on the front of whatever unstylish outfit I was wearing.

I guess that other than the night I was born, this was the biggest night in Penticton's history. The next day, Monday, May 17, 1954, the *Penticton Herald* actually published a six-page extra, whose banner declared in huge caps: "PROUDLY WE HAIL THE GREAT PENTICTON V'S—1954 ALLAN CUP CHAMPIONS." There were the usual shots on the front page, including mugging with the trophy, and the other pages were devoted to pictures and descriptions of the team's members. Under each photo was a reminder of the services offered by outfits such as Emerald Cleaners and Vet's Taxi.

I often thank the poetry gods that I was in the right time and place to learn poetry from the right elders and peers. Back in the day when I was still a hockey fan, I was similarly lucky to have been caught up in what no one thought of calling Vee-mania. The heart (and playing manager) of this team from a place the Toronto hockey scribes had never heard of was the wonderful veteran Grant Warwick. "Knobby" Warwick, we all knew, was a big-league forward. He had won the Calder Trophy as the NHL's best rookie in 1942, a year after winning his first Allan Cup with some Saskatchewan team. There were a lot of guys his age fighting a war in Europe during those years, but we all knew that there was some good reason that Warwick was holding a hockey stick instead of a Lee-Enfield.

Warwick patrolled, as the sportswriters say, right wing for the New York Rangers for seven years, making it onto the first ever NHL All-Star Team in 1947 and scoring a goal against the Maple Leafs. Then he got traded to Boston, and a year later became a Montreal Canadien. After a year with them he was back in the American Hockey League, where he skated for two seasons (do you see the pattern? Nowadays in the era of big money, it doesn't happen anymore) before going back to senior hockey in the Maritimes, and, a year later, to the Okanagan. With the Vees he was a yearly all-star, and still in his mid-thirties.

The Warwick brothers became B.C. hockey's version of the Younger Brothers. It was taken for granted that if anyone bopped diminutive Dickie Warwick in the course of his labours, his two older brothers, whether they were on the ice, on the bench, or already in the penalty box, would land on that foe like a cyclone of sticks and skates. The Warwicks were mean, clannish, thuggish at times, not good examples for the youth of the day, according to the mothers of the youth. But man, they were exciting!

Grant Warwick, the clan leader, got 79 points and 79 penalty minutes in that marvellous 1953–54 season. But his brother Bill just tore the league apart that year. In 58 regular season games he got 50 goals, 95 points and 127 minutes in penalties, to lead the OSAHL in all those categories. Though Grant had his decade in the NHL, and Bill played for minor professional teams all over the United States, little Dickie had only five games as a professional before coming to play centre in Penticton.

We told each other lots of stories about the Warwick brothers, and we hung out at the Commodore Café until the waitresses in their little "Go V's" hats glared at us concerning the need for our table. The Warwicks owned the popular café, and one of the stories we told each other was that little Dickie, who was supposed to have Saint Vitus's dance, made the cakes for their dessert menu. The main story about Grant was that he was a big drinker. We swore to one another that we had seen him hanging onto a lamppost outside the restaurant in the middle of the night.

I don't remember being loose on Main Street up in Penticton during the middle of the night.

But the most interesting stories were about Bill Warwick. Everybody in the league was supposed to be afraid of the Warwicks and their crashing bashing hockey, but they were mainly afraid of Billy. At both ends of Memorial Arena, the end boards were either noticeably new or scarred like crazy. This was supposed to be because once Billy got up to high speed he didn't really know how to stop, except by smashing into the end boards. Adding to the fright factor was the fact that Billy transmogrified as the game went on. For one thing, he was the only guy in the league wearing a helmet. The only other hockey player I have seen wearing the kind of helmet he wore was the poet Fred Wah, who played town hockey in the Kootenays. This helmet resembled those things that cyclists used to wear, something that looked like parallel leather ropes, hair showing between them.

Now here is the other thing about that helmet. During his first shift or two, Bill Warwick just looked like an angry gorilla in a funny headpiece slamming his way up the ice, bouncing off anything that did not get out of his way. But by the end of the first period, his face would be drained of colour, as if his blood were hiding. He would come to resemble a horror-movie creature with his weird hat and his pure white face. Between the first and second periods, we used to tell each other, not believing this story now, the trainer would put Bill in a cage and throw raw meat in after him.

But we did pretty well believe the story about Billy's white face. Unlike Grant, we said, Bill did not drink, and here was why: back in his junior hockey days on the prairie, Billy and four of his teammates were riding in a fast car toward the town where they were supposed to play a game the next night. They were all teenagers and they were all drunk, and eventually there was a horrible crash. All the other lads were killed, and Bill was in hospital for months, a pile of broken bones and injured organs. They had to put a plate in his skull, and his face was rebuilt by plastic surgery. Us kids thought that had something to do with plastic, a commodity that had only in recent years entered our lives.

Anyway, that was why Bill Warwick didn't drink, and that was why his face went white and scared the bejesus out of hapless Kelowna Packers and Vernon Canadians.

Of course I don't believe that story now.

The big bad Warwicks. While they were terrorizing mothers' sons on Okanagan ice (and Kootenay ice, during interleague games), the East York Lyndhursts were in Stockholm, cruising their way toward a World Ice Hockey Championship. In those days it was generally thought that you could send a dozen Canadian amputees to the tournament and win games by 20 goals. But something happened in March 1954 that would rattle the soul of Canadian hockey. Canada had won 14 of the first 15 tournaments, but the Senior B league East York Lyndhursts had a surprise waiting for them in Sweden. The Soviet Union was in the tournament for the first time, and in a sign of things to come, faced Canada in the championship game.

The Soviets were fast, accurate and disciplined. They trounced the Lyndhursts 7–2, or as a lot of sportswriters in Canada had it, the Communists with their lack of individuality shocked the free world and its free skaters. I remember the panic that swept through the Canadian hockey world, or at least through the press and broadcasters. The Cold War was really getting cold when upstarts from outside the world could come in and steal our game. The Korean "police action" had come to a non-end in July 1953. Eastern Europe was freezing behind the iron curtain. The self-respect of the free world relied on the skates and sticks of hockeyists who were not quite good enough to play in the NHL.

Something had to be done to show the world that democratic Canada was the proper home of the game. Now, those Russkies were pretty good, probably because they were robots controlled from the Kremlin. Most of them were members of the Red Army, the same outfit that kept Eastern Europe and a lot of Asian "republics" in check. Who could stand up to them? Why, the rough and ready Penticton Vees, the tough guys who had won a miracle Allan Cup against the best that Eastern Canada could put up against them! Canada asked Grant Warwick to take his bully boys over to Dusseldorf for the 1955 World Championship tournament and reignite the flame of Canadian pride.

That's the kind of language you heard a lot in the fifties. Many headlines had the word "REDS" in them. Penticton was 40 miles from the U.S. border, in a fruit-growing valley that extended south through Washington state. Canada wholeheartedly joined with the USA in its animus against the Commies. Grant Warwick knew what his mission was.

And he knew how to succeed. He was a veteran of the so-called hockey wars, and he knew how his wild bunch could make a mess of the effete Europeans. The Russians and the Swedes and the Norwegians were Europe. They were the intellectual snobs who looked on new world folks as lumberjacks and miners. Warwick decided that his ruffians would play feeling against thinking, emotion against intellect, bare fists against team tactics.

The Vees went to Europe early and played eight exhibition games before the tournament. Now the German public and others got to see what we had seen in the rinks of the Okanagan league. And they did not like it. The Vees would start the rough stuff at the opening whistle, and send innocent men into or over the boards. The choreographed tactics of the European teams would be disrupted by bodychecks legal and illegal, and when Canadians dropped their gloves to signal a readiness to duke it out, the Europeans would skate away, earning the scorn of the brutish visitors. Meanwhile the rinks would be filled with the sustained whistling of the fans, who hated to see hockey reduced to idiotic violence. The

European newspapers reviled the Canadians, and some of the Canadian reporters agreed with them, though their language might have been more evasive.

Whoever made up the tournament schedule knew what they were doing. Canada was slotted in to play the Soviets on the last day. On the way to that game, this is what the Canadians did:

Canada	12	USA	1
Canada	5	Czechoslovakia	3
Canada	8	Poland	0
Canada	12	Finland	0
Canada	11	Switzerland	1
Canada	3	Sweden	0
Canada	10	West Germany	1

Playing almost every day, Penticton's skinny goalie Ivan McLelland had given up only six goals in seven games.

Meanwhile, the defending champions had done pretty well with their fast and graceful game:

USSR	10	Finland	2
USSR	2	Sweden	1
USSR	4	Czechoslovakia	0
USSR	8	Poland	2
USSR	3	USA	0
USSR	5	West Germany	1
USSR	7	Switzerland	2

The Warwicks and the rest of the Canadians had a game plan for the Soviet encounter. Smash someone as soon as the puck hit the ice in the first period, and continue the mayhem. The German crowd whistled like crazy, dropping all loyalty to NATO and cheering for the Russkies. But Grant's mob bashed and slammed, and the Red Army guys were seen to be avoiding checks and shying away from goalmouth pileups. Grant Warwick, exhausted after 16 games in 19 days said, ungraciously, "They quit on us." Ivan McLelland got his fourth shutout and Bill Warwick scored two goals as the Vees won it 5–0. Despite his 0.75 goals against record, McLelland finished behind the USAmerican in the voting for best goalie of the tournament. Bill Warwick was best forward with his 14 goals and eight assists.

I got to see the game.

I had joined the Royal Canadian Air Force a few weeks after drinking from the Allan Cup. I went to Saint-Jean-sur-Richelieu in Quebec for basic training that summer, then to Camp Borden for my trade training as an aerial photographer. I finished first in my class and was thus given my choice of the available postings. Well, I would have had first choice, except that there was a married guy in my class, and he got to jump the queue. He picked Comox on Vancouver Island. I have been kicking myself for years and years for the choice I made. I could have had a Prince Edward Island station that had the nickname "Overseas Squadron" because they spent part of the year in the Caribbean. But I was an 18-year-old moron. I went for the farthest west station still available—Macdonald, Manitoba.

In the late fall of 1954, I took a train to Portage la Prairie, and somehow found the RCAF bus that travelled the 18 miles between that little city and my new air force base. I thought that I would get a good look at the Manitoba prairie on the way there. Here is what I saw: the occasional bit of highway pavement as the wind momentarily blew the drifting snow off it. When I got to RCAF Macdonald, they outfitted me with some big zippered rubber boots, whose toes I eventually spray-painted yellow to distinguish them from the hundreds of other pairs in the mud room of the mess hall.

My fellow photographers at the photo section gave me the nickname "Babyface," perhaps because I seldom had to use my service-issue razor. I told them I was from Penticton, because I didn't want them to think I came from a Podunkville place downriver called Oliver. They might not even have known about Penticton if the Vees hadn't won the Senior Championship of Canada. When my "hometown" team hammered its way through all the European and U.S. opposition in Germany, I was not a quiet rookie around the photo section or anywhere else on the base.

So when the Soviet-Canada game was shown on the mess hall television set on Monday, March 7, the sergeant in charge of my section gave me half a day off to go and watch my guys clobber the Russkies.

This was not your colour TV.

This was not your flat-screen HDTV.

This was not your replay, close-up, stop-action, reverse-angle TV.

This was not even your "live" TV. The game had been played the day before. We knew that Bill Warwick was going to wave his stick in the face of some guy whose name ended the same way a lot of Manitoba farmers' names ended, and that the Vees were going to win 5–0 and regain ice hockey honour for our nation. We had been up at six in the morning, listening to Foster Hewitt yell and scream on CBC radio.

As a matter of fact, the CBC television network had just a month or so earlier reached its coaxial cable into the Keystone Province. The kinescope of the big game had been flown from Dusseldorf to Toronto the day before, and it was by great good fortune that we got to watch the game so soon.

Oh, and just to continue a theme that has developed as if by itself, I should mention some individual measurements here. To put one of them into perspective, I will mention that there was a Bill Warwick born in 1897, who became a catcher in the National League of baseball. He was six feet tall and weighed 180 pounds when he crouched for the Pittsburgh Pirates. In 1955 the monstrous Bill Warwick who caused opposition skaters to reconsider hobbies was all of 5-foot-7 and 165 pounds. He towered over his brother Grant Warwick, who was 5-foot-6 and weighed 155. Their little brother Dickie was always putting himself in the way of tough guys, so his big brothers came to his rescue. He was a shade shorter than his brothers, and weighed 145 pounds.

Oh, and when I drank from the Allan Cup? I was a little over 6-foot-2.

The Penticton Vees went into a gradual decline after the World Championship. In fact the whole Okanagan Senior Amateur Hockey League lasted only six more years. The Vernon Canadians won the last championship in 1961. The

CBC Television network reached British Columbia by 1956, and in 1957 there was a CBC-TV station in Kelowna. It was not long until people in the South Okanagan were getting signals from the USA. In just the way that franchise store malls would kill local retail and restaurants, creating monstrosities like today's Kelowna, television in the late fifties and early sixties killed local sports organizations. That's what happened to the Okanagan Mainline Baseball League. Nowadays the world of sports in the Okanagan Valley means golf. New golf courses go up in the hills, another sign that where we once read "sports" we should now read "business."

There is still some ice hockey in the Valley, and there is still a little baseball, but we are talking about junior hockey and Little League baseball. If you want to see grown-ups play, well, you can watch television.

ONTARIO
AGAIN

After the air force I went back to university, at UBC. While there I watched some football games, because I worked in the UBC library Saturday mornings, and the Thunderbirds' home games were played early on Saturday afternoons. The experience was not at all like college football in Hollywood movies, though UBC played U.S. rules in a U.S. conference. I was usually sitting with about 150 other galoots, many of whom were emptying mickeys of whiskey or rum and tossing them noisily behind their heels and down below the stands. We cheered derisively as the Thunderbirds strove to stay within three touchdowns of the squad from Western Washington College in Bellingham.

There was a semi-pro basketball league around in those days, some of the players from the ranks of the B.C. Lions football team, and I caught a few of their games. I particularly recall the skill of Emery Barnes. He was an all-around athlete who played football for the University of Oregon and was a reserve high jumper on the 1952 U.S. Olympic team. He played two games in the National Football League, then joined the B.C. Lions. I watched him play football and basketball. I got to see him and Willie Fleming, the great running back, when I was in the hospital and they came to visit someone. I was lucky enough to live in B.C. when Barnes was elected to the Legislative Assembly of British Columbia as a social democrat. He won the Order of British Columbia years before I did, and he died earlier than such a good man should.

So while I was a student at UBC, I got to see football games and AAA baseball games contested by the late lamented Vancouver Mounties, but I did not go to hockey games, though if I was near a TV set I got to see the Toronto Maple Leafs and Montreal Canadiens in their black and white uniforms. The Vancouver Canucks played in the Western Hockey League, but they never caught the public fancy as their NHL successors have. I did not see kids with hockey sticks getting on the bus, or portable goalie nets on the streets of residential areas. Only after the Canucks got into the NHL in 1970 did hockey catch on with kids and their parents.

When I came back to Vancouver in 1971, I saw lots of kids with hockey sticks. Most of them were right-hand shots, just the opposite of what you would see in Quebec and Ontario, where boys start to play ice hockey while wearing onesies. I went into a sports equipment store in my neighbourhood and asked a salesperson whether this meant that most west coast kids were left-handed. No, he told me, the right-hand sticks sold so well because in this new hockey territory, most of the equipment was bought by mothers who thought that because their kids were right-handed they needed right-hand sticks.

Maybe it was one of those mothers that designed the Canadian five-dollar bill with the winter sports scenes on the back. It depicts five kids playing outdoor hockey, and they are all right-handed shots. Must be playing somewhere around Vancouver, in the rain.

One of my best friends during my UBC days was Lionel Kearns. He, like me, was a tyro poet, but he was also a saxophonist and a hockey player. He had grown up in Nelson while I was growing up in Oliver, so he knew about snow and ice and ice skates. He once told me that he quit playing junior hockey when his coach told him to go out there and injure a good player on the other team. But you could not get hockey out of Lionel's blood. In 1965, when we were in Mexico City together, he took me down to the ice-hockey arena, where he and his West Kootenay pal Bill Horswill had played as Canadian imports on an *équipe de hockey sobre hielo* several years earlier. In fact the last I heard, Lionel was one of the younger forwards on an over-75 ice hockey team. That's years.

Anyway, by 1965 I was living and teaching in Calgary, where I went to a few football games played by the then-hapless Stampeders, but never watched a live hockey game, even though they had been playing hockey in Calgary since the 1890s. Perhaps I would have gone to watch the Stampeders of the Western Hockey League, but they folded a few months before we came to town. The Alberta Junior Hockey League started that year, but the two Calgary teams never caught my interest. And in 1966, we loaded our old Chevy with clothes and books and moved to London, Ontario.

It was the first time I had lived in Ontario since 1954. The main difference between Alberta and Ontario is that in Ontario the snow is not as dry. Oh, and this was before Alberta had taken over Canada's governance from Ontario, so my first wife Angela and I felt a little like bashful Westerners in the home counties of the empire.

"This is where real hockey is played," I told her.

London was the new home of the Toronto Maple Leafs' second junior team in the Ontario Hockey Association. In those days the six teams in the NHL operated the junior amateur teams, stocking them with prospects and keeping Canada's winter game alive in Ontario's towns, giving people in places such as Kitchener and Niagara Falls something to live for. Toronto's other OHA Junior A team was the Toronto Marlboros.

Junior hockey around London was really confusing in those days. Junior B hockey kept moving in and out of town, and in a couple years the London Nationals would be the London Knights, the Junior A league would get bigger and bigger, and the Junior B team would get named the Nationals, and so on. But Junior A was the real deal in southern Ontario. A year after we left, the London Nationals would get young Darryl Sittler for three years, and the Leafs' future captain would be my second favourite Leaf to wear my favourite number.

[Please note: I am now going to depart from an orderly narrative to flash back to the late fifties, and I am going to write something about sex, so you readers who just want hockey and no hoohaw should skip forward a few paragraphs.]

My first favourite Leaf to wear my favourite number, which is 27, by the way, was Frank Mahovlich. In 1957–58, he was a rookie with the Maple Leafs, and at the end of the season he won the Calder Trophy as the best rookie in the league. I was two years older than he, but when it came to going all the way, as we said in my day, I was just past my rookie year myself. My virginity had managed to disappear not long before I departed the RCAF, and in the season of 1957–58 I was a sophomore at UBC.

I was very lucky that year to know a Trinidadian student who was voluptuous and female and good-natured. She would go on to marry the aforementioned Lionel Kearns, and become the mother of a hockey-playing son in North Vancouver. But her importance here is that she had a friend who was a grade 12 tennis-playing student at Lord Byng High School, and I was lucky enough to be introduced to this beautiful blonde girl with the racquet in her hand. I don't know how it happened, but soon this lovely creature and I were an item.

She was one of those somewhat privileged girls who leaned toward such sports as tennis, scuba diving and boating. Even though I was a small-town supporter of the working class, I enjoyed the new life I found myself in, wearing my $30 suit at the opera and getting my picture taken with patrons of the arts. It was complicated. I fancied myself a writer and a rough-hewn intellectual, but I was abashed trying to learn how to use the salt when we went to dinner at the home of her grandmother, who came from a famous musical family in central Europe.

So while I learned how to operate a boat on the edge of the ocean and up the Fraser River, I taught her five-pin bowling. And while we were studying and otherwise sharing her apartment, I introduced her to the worlds of Major League Baseball, the Canadian Football League and the NHL.

[I am trying to think of a way to describe the following event with some delicacy, and I have even thought of leaving it out of this book, but the lives of Frank Mahovlich and me were tendentiously intertwined for many years, and life is in the end a conduit to literature, isn't it?]

I was madly in love with this adorable creature whose name I am hearing in my head right now. She studied theatre and showed me what to read about it. She could draw and paint and sculpt and dance. She was good at all the arts except the written ones, which were my bailiwick, and the musical ones, which were her family's. She had a nice speaking voice, and a pretty face, with green eyes and freckles. And she had, well it was the late fifties, a body that we idiot lads usually had to dream about.

So, to get to the story—one early Saturday evening we were making love at her apartment, and I had the radio on, tuned to *Hockey Night in Canada*, of course. Things got pretty exciting as the play went back and forth, and I don't care whether you believe me, but Frank Mahovlich had the puck and was making one of his famous rinklength rushes, and when Foster Hewitt said "He shoots! He scores!" well, so did I.

In later years I would see Frank Mahovlich play for the Montreal Canadiens and the Birmingham Bulls. You will remember that for a while he was my travel agent when

I went to do poetry readings in places such as Inuvik and Sherbrooke. And yes, when I was made the Parliamentary Poet Laureate I visited the Canadian Senate, and looking down from the visitors' perch I saw that he was the only senator there with a head of black hair. On further visits I noticed that while most senators were not in their seats, Mahovlich always was.

Now, back to London, Ontario. The other future star who shone for the locals was Garry Unger. He too would go on to skate well at centre for the Maple Leafs, though he would be a St. Louis Blue for his peak years. For a long time he was known as the league's ironman, having played 914 consecutive games, but his position would be usurped by the likeable 5-foot-9 Doug Jarvis, who played 50 more.

Doug Jarvis was younger but Garry was Unger. Doug never had something that Garry apparently had galore. Garry was cute. At least that is what a small group of gay men I knew told me over and over. I don't know what percentage of gay men watch NHL hockey games on television, but these guys would make stupendous claims for the ardour with which they pined for the playmaker with the streaming blond hair.

As I have said, I did not see any junior hockey games during the year that we lived in London, Ont. But I had two hockey experiences. One of them involved a person whose name I had heard all through my adolescent years—Turk Broda. When I was a kid "officially afflicted with the Toronto Maple Leafs," Turk Broda was their colourful goalie. He was a perfect guy for the age, a combination of superior skill and comic looks in the mould of Lou Costello and Yogi Berra.

You might say that he was a little dumpy. His boss

Conn Smythe certainly did, and tried all kinds of threats and inducements to make him lose poundage. The newspapers called this "The Battle of the Bulge." Eventually Turk slimmed enough to satisfy Smythe, and frustrate the best forwards in the NHL. He was between the pipes, as they say, when the Maple Leafs became the only team in any sport to come from behind three games to none and win a playoff series 4–3. This happened, you'll recall, against the Detroit Red Wings in the spring of 1942, when Turk won his first of many Stanley Cups.

For reasons that you know, I never got to see Turk Broda play hockey. But during that winter in London, Ont., I got to see him at his other favourite activity—eating.

I don't remember the name of the street, maybe Dundas, and I don't remember the name of the place—it was one of those little modern joints—but I remember walking by the front corner window, and here is what I saw: my old childhood hero Turk Broda sitting alone at a small table, looking down at what had just been placed on it—a plate upon which rested nothing but an enormous beef steak, a steak so big that its marbled boundaries hung down a little outside the perimeter of the plate. The battle of the bulge had been lost, or was it won? Six years later he died of a heart attack, aged 58.

Before I tell you about my second hockey experience that year in Southwest Ontario, I have another not-so-great hockey poem to lay on you. It was published in *Points on the Grid*, which was my first real (i.e., published in Toronto) book, in 1964, while I was still living in Calgary, not going to hockey games but watching them on black-and-white television:

The Hockey Hero

                            faces a shifting field
of action   men on skates   leaving him only
moments of pathway   a dash to left or right
a closing

               HE MUST BANG THE THING IN!
               or a
banging rebound!
               quick roar of   the crowd

               And faces a clattering
               moment's trellis of sticks
               poking for
               the thing
               in the corner

  And the long pushing rush to the other end
to catch the man with the   puck
now on his stick
               the meeting
               impact the
               crash against the boards

And the thing sliding free ahead
               a second's maze of men
               a pickup and a
BANGING REBOUND!

You could have inferred one or more things from this poem of youth.

1. The poet was no hockey player, or
2. The young man had a lot to learn about poetry, and/or
3. Hockey, unlike baseball, does not provide inspiration or material for much poetry.

Well, some of my poet friends did play hockey, Lionel Kearns, as you know, and Fred Wah, both of them from the West Kootenays, where ice would accumulate in the winter months. Lionel is currently playing with a leg injury that he sustained by tripping over the blue line a few years ago. That's what he says. As for Fred Wah—quite a few years ago I functioned as timekeeper and bell-clanger in a house-league game he was playing against some outfit from Trail. I was impressed by how tall he looked in his skates and by the Bill Warwick-style helmet he wore.

Fred has always had a little bit of a mean streak in him, which hockey players are supposed to have and let loose in strategic times. In a house league of fairly old guys, maybe not so much. I do remember that as Fred and I rode off in the snow before the game, his wife, Pauline, warned him that she was not going to pay any more of his fines.

So, to the second hockey experience in the 1966–67 season. We got to London, Ont., where I would be pursuing my Ph.D. in late September, stayed for a week at the Maple Glen Motel, then moved with our dogs into our rented house on October 1. The NHL season would start on October 19, so there wasn't much time left in the pre-season. You will remember that back then the big-league teams had farms in the OHA, so pre-season was a good time for ordinary people to survey the stars in shorts and garter belts. The New York Rangers had their kids playing for the Kitchener Rangers, whom I had seen 12 years earlier when they were the Guelph Biltmore Mad Hatters. The Boston Bruins had moved their kids from Niagara Falls to Oshawa, and in the spring of 1966, a kid named Bobby Orr almost led the Generals to the junior championship, but Edmonton would beat them and the groin-injured Orr for the Memorial Cup.

In the fall of 1966, Bobby Orr was a rookie for the Bruins, an 18-year-old with a preposterously high salary pried from the Bruins by Orr's agent, the beneficent Alan Eagleson. The Bruins played a pre-season game against the New York Rangers in Kitchener, Ontario, and among the Rangers forwards was a guy with a crooked nose and thick black hair, who was nearly twice Orr's age at that time. This was Bernie "Boom Boom" Geoffrion, inventor and perfecter of the slapshot, a native of Montreal, and one of the greatest of the Montreal Canadiens' great forwards until the year in question.

Geoffrion may have been the most exciting player the Habs had ever had, if you equate exciting with ominous and erotic. I hasten to mention that he was 5-foot-9 and appeared to be made of muscular steel. He would go on to become a coach in the NHL, but coaches are not supposed to be mobile explosions. "Boom Boom" was a right winger who looked as if he might take your head off with his shot or his teeth. I am saying that he was not a gentle scholar. His first female ancestor in Quebec was a King's daughter, if you know what that is. He was a beautiful son of a gun.

Bobby Orr was an offence-minded defenceman who

played mainly on the left side, so he would get to know Bernie Geoffrion quite well in this game in Kitchener.

Oh, and what I meant to say is that my wife and I were at this game. It was the first game I had ever seen in which major league teams played each other. Like everyone else in Canada, I was eager to see how this newly rich teenager was going to do in that kind of competition. A lot of NHL players were mad at Orr already, because his rookie salary was higher than their veterans' salaries. I was also taken with the fact that the number on his back was 27— my favourite, as you know.

My wife was not a regular hockey fan, though she did know quite a few of the expressions one uses while watching hockey on television. "You stupid asshole! Pass the gad damned puck!" for example. For whatever reason, it was not long until she became, let us say, an avid supporter of the Rangers' offence. She thought that Red Berenson was a more than capable centre, and Rod Gilbert was a pretty exciting skater. Reggie Fleming was pretty solid, and Bob Nevin could bring it. But she was, I could tell, most fully impressed by Bernie Geoffrion. In fact, even though I informed her that he was way older than I, she was quite willing to discuss him.

"Who do you like the best on the ice so far?" I asked after the first period.

"Boom Boom," was her answer.

"That Bobby Orr looks as if he is going to be able to handle himself," I said.

"Boom Boom," she said. "On the ice."

"I wish we had seen him 10 years ago," I put in.

"Or on the floor," she added.

"He's still a strong skater at his age," I continued.

"The barn floor!" she said, and her eyes were not really looking in my direction. "Or the ground outside the barn!"

I went for popcorn and Coke.

I don't remember who won the game, nor how many points young Orr or old Geoffrion got, but I felt that I had at last added another experience to my life. I have never gone to as many sports events, musical shows, or other entertainment events as most people seem to do, but I always savour the experience fully. My first NBA game transpired between the Pistons and the Lakers, in the Winnipeg Arena when I was in the RCAF. The Lakers were playing some of their home games away from their regular base because they weren't drawing enough fans in Minneapolis. I can't remember whether they beat Fort Wayne that night. I heard Cream play from their album *Disraeli Gears* in the hockey arena in Calgary during the summer of 1968. I went with my wife and daughter to the Kirov Ballet Theatre in St. Petersburg in 1984. The NHL exhibition game in Kitchener was my sports moment until less than a year later when I went with my lacrosse-playing buddy, the painter Greg Curnoe, to my first big-league baseball game in Detroit early in the 1967 season.

But we are here to talk about hockey, not baseball. I would like to say something about baseball players, though. How can you tell that baseball players are smarter than hockey players? Baseball teams never get penalized for having too many players on the field.

EROS *and* FASHION

So, we have seen that Garry Unger was the erotic choice of gay men, and that Bernie Geoffrion was the erotic choice of married women. Over the years I have made casual research of this topic, not restricting my area to the sport of ice hockey. In fact, ice hockey, it would seem to me, forgetting about hockey sticks and overtime and so on, would be an unlikely choice for the sexual fancy. Around the time of Geoffrion and Unger, basketball players cavorted in outfits that resembled underwear more than anything else. The shorts were almost short shorts or hot pants, and pretty tight. The singlets were form-fitting. And the tall tube socks were also seen to be very popular in porn films. In other words, the players' duds were almost indistinguishable from those worn by the cheerleaders.

Sports fashions tend to imitate street fashions. Back in the day (see the Beatles) suits were tight, lapels were narrow and fedoras had tiny brims. Of course women struggled into miniskirts, and nearby men tended to drop things. But then along came hip-hop, and baggy pants and bling to go along with the stupid song lyrics, and before you knew it, NBA shorts looked more like ankle-length culottes. Eroticism pretty well disappeared, replaced by the loud rap music that now fills NBA arenas.

Baseball uniforms in the sixties were pretty snug, too. Everyone tried to look the way Alfonso Soriano would look a few decades later at Yankee Stadium and Wrigley, a slender body tightly wrapped in cloth that seemed to fondle his baseball muscles. Unfortunately, baseball uniforms would feature one of the worst things to happen to men's clothing in the seventies—double knit fabric. This was especially unfortunate for the more rotund managers and coaches of the time—think Don Zimmer.

I have often thought about the fact that baseball is the only sport that makes the managers and coaches wear the uniforms their players wear. Connie Mack never managed in anything but his really old-fashioned suit, and in recent times Terry Francona has found ways to be only half in uniform. But here is what I was thinking: what if basketball managers and coaches had to wear shorts, singlets and sneakers? What if football coaches had to be in uniform, including helmets? And how about making hockey coaches wear full team-gear, including gloves, helmets and skates?

But that is a serious argument to be made elsewhere. Here we are talking about the sexiness of athletic outfits. I have often heard women (and a few men) exclaim approvingly about the skin-tightness of football pants, especially just before the snap. Boxing would seem attractive to those who like to see men wearing only gloves, shoes and shorts, especially if they are sweating a lot and getting hit often. Except in Muslim countries, track-and-field outfits and swimsuits are becoming more minimal with the years.

But what do ice hockey players wear? I have a theory that there is a lot of fighting in hockey games because of what these young men have to wear, what with garter belts and the like.

First you have to put on a pair of long johns. This is a good time to walk through the dressing room to take a pee. Then if you like socks inside your skates, put on a pair of socks so thin you'll be able to feel the skates against your skin. Then strap on your jockstrap and stick your protective cup inside it. Don't worry about having to undo all this to have a leak during the game. You will be sweating so much liquid you won't need a leak. Now it's time to put that garter belt on. Then, if your shin guards have straps, tighten them before you start yarding those hockey stockings up. This would be a good time to be thankful that you are not living in the old days, when socks were thick and scratchy wool. Okay, yank those colourful socks until they reach well up on your thighs. Then wrap tape around the tops twice and stick them to your long johns, then wrap tape around your legs just under your knees so that your shin guards will stay snug. Now step into your padded hockey shorts and get their suspenders over your shoulders. The suspenders don't have to match the garter belt in colour. Now it is time to sit down and lace up your skates. Remember, two little bunny ears. Next it is time for your elbow pads. Hooray for Velcro.

Then that thing that is partly shoulder pads and partly breast protector. Get it over your head and adjust it nice and tight. Pull your jersey over your head with the number toward the back. Now you are ready for your helmet. If it has a face guard, this goes in front. Snap the chin strap. Slip in your mouth guard. Finally, put your gloves on and grab your hockey stick. You are ready to clump out of the dressing room and onto the ice. Life is good.

You might even forget that you are wearing a garter belt. If not, remember that that tough guy that wants to drop the gloves and be a man is wearing one, too.

And remember—most hockey fans have been brain-washed since childhood. They don't even think there is something funny about wearing shorts over high stockings with coloured rings around them.

In the 1981–82 season, two NHL teams tossed the shorts and went with long pants, the Philadelphia Flyers with orange ones and the Hartford Whalers with green ones. Several junior hockey teams followed (uh) suit. It looked pretty slick and grown-up. Slick was the bad word. Players found out that if you fell or got knocked down at high speed, you would slide really fast right into the boards or pipes. Lots of players who had trouble keeping to their feet complained about this feature of their game. Lots of hockey fans complained because, well, it was something new. These hockey fans also complained when the Vancouver Canucks came onto the ice with no isolated logo on their chests but rather a design that could have been construed as a V. Anyway, after the 1982–83 season there were no more long pants in the NHL, except those on the referees and coaches.

BECOMING
an **HABITANT**

We moved to Montreal in 1967. The first thing I learned from the anglophones there, most of whom were Jewish, was that you don't say "Mawntreal." You say "Muntreal." The other day I heard my brother, who is a lifelong Habs fan but who has never been back east, say "Mawntreal." I corrected him, of course. At least, unlike Foster Hewitt, he sort of knew how to say Cornoyer.

Montreal was the host city for the 1967 World's Fair, called *Terre des hommes*, the nickname taken from the 1939 book by Antoine de Saint-Exupéry. Maybe the anglophones were thinking of his name when they called the fair Expo 67. So when we got there it was pretty darn hard to find an apartment. We had to choose between a six-room flat above a store on Greene Avenue and a seven-and-a-half-room flat in lower Westmount. We took the latter and lived there for four years, never settling the question of which was the half-room.

In 1969, the Montreal Expos were born, and for two years I would live the dream of abiding in a Major League Baseball city, though it felt kind of bush going to ball games in a picayune stadium of aluminum seats and no covered grandstand. But in 1967, major league hockey started skating on slushy ice. The NHL, fearing the rumours of plans for a second league, and hoping to make some television money in the U.S., doubled its size. Not only did the league directors add six teams; they mandated that one of the six new teams would play one of the "Original Six" teams in the Stanley Cup Finals.

What happened in the 1967–68 Stanley Cup Finals? As everyone expected, the Montreal Canadiens beat the St. Louis Blues in four games straight. What no one expected was that the Blues would lose each of those games by one goal. Montreal goalie Gump Worsley won 11 straight games in the 1968 playoffs, but Glenn Hall was in the St. Louis net. Hall had won the Vezina Trophy with Chicago the year before, but he was 36 years old, so the Black Hawks didn't protect him during the expansion draft. A year later he had the Canadiens cursing bilingually for four games. In one of those games, Montreal outshot the Blues 46 to 15, as one might have expected in a match between the most storied champions in hockey history and an expansion team from the U.S. Midwest. Glenn Hall won the playoffs' Conn Smythe Trophy while playing for a team that did not win the Stanley Cup. That does not happen often, though it should, perhaps, happen more often than it does.

So there I was in Montreal—the only male in my

family who did not cheer for the Canadiens. But at last I was going to get to see the best hockey in the world, at least this side of Moscow. I had seen that one pre-season game the year before, but it had been played in a Podunk arena in Ontario. Now I got to join those fabled fans who attended greatness in the Forum, as if it were a birthright. So what was to be my very first regular season NHL experience? Just wait a couple of paragraphs.

In the summer of 1968, the Forum underwent renovations, as they say. The 1960s saw a lot of massive building on the so-called island of Montreal and environs, including Expo 67, the central Place Bonaventure, the cruciform Place Ville-Marie, the Métro, the Décarie Expressway, the Champlain Bridge, et cetera et cetera. The expansion of the Forum, in most Montrealers' minds the most important building in town, led the way to a bigger more impressive city, and would even prepare the scene for the Olympics of eight years later. Montreal would never regain its position as Canada's biggest city, and it would no longer have to rely on dubious claims of sporting the best restaurants and entertainment sites. This was a city with giant architectural dreams.

On August 19, 1968, in order to acquire a physical reminder of this building boom and its exaltation, Angela and I, along with Jennifer, the model who lived across the hall from us on Grosvenor Avenue, went under the cover of night and liberated a few bricks from the Forum work site. I am sort of glad that my souvenir got lost in one of my many moves, because the place is now named the Pepsi Forum and is called an "entertainment and retail complex." As to the Bell Centre, current home of the

Canadiens—I don't think you'll ever find me there. And as for souvenirs? I still have my Hartford Whalers puck.

So, I bought myself a birthday present, a ticket to the game of November 30, 1967, the night before my 31st birthday. The visiting team was the Minnesota North Stars. The final score was 1–1.

Is this all there is? I asked myself on the way home on the crowded, overheated number 10 bus.

Still, I was pulling in $12,000 a year as writer-in-residence at Sir George Williams University. I could sometimes spare a couple dollars and a few hours for a hockey game, especially if I got to go to the Forum with my new friend, the erudite and amusing novelist and especially short-story writer Hugh Hood. Hugh used to yell things such as, "You can have the shower, but we want our Kurtenbach." Hockey fans will get it and clap for more, as I did.

I was, remember, officially afflicted with the Toronto Maple Leafs, so I went to the Forum to cheer against the team in the glowing white jerseys and blue shorts. As the long Montreal fall turned into the even longer Montreal winter, it got darker and darker, until it was dark on the way to the game. From the window of the number 10 bus I saw an outdoor skating rink with boards around it and lights hanging over it and boys in toques skating back and forth with Sher-Woods in their hands. And as winter deepened, it became less and less possible to cheer against the Canadiens. How could a person sit there, or more often stand there, and see Henri Richard break up the ice and take a just barely on-side pass from J.C. Tremblay and menace the awakening Detroit goalie, and not feel a rush of *jouissance*? When the Canadiens headmanned the puck, and the roar from 18,000 Montrealers echoed against itself in the legendary Forum, a big C with a smaller capital H in its grasp would magically appear on my chest.

How could I, a boy who swore lifetime loyalty to the blue and white, add my anglo voice to that roar? Years later, when I stood next to Donatello's *Magdalene* for the third time, I leaned against the wall and wept. When I felt my body wrapped in the sound created by the throng screaming its love for their hockey immortals, I opened my mouth and made elemental noise. The vocal support was not, as far as I could tell, arranged by any class system. In the lower level of seats there were fashionable men in suits and chapeaus and ties and polished leather shoes, and there were women in furs and Italian footwear. In the middle section were people in decent slacks and overcoats. In the top section were guys in bomber jackets and women in bellbottom jeans. They all acted as if Jean Béliveau had skated here from Elysium.

When you were in the Forum, you knew how lucky you were. This was the most important building in the world of ice hockey. Everyone knew that. Even though kids like me stuck their ears to the prairie radio and imagined ourselves in Maple Leaf Gardens, and even though there were childbirths and murders in the big dark edifice in Chicago, the building on Saint Catherine at Atwater was the shrine, the epicentre, the place from whose high rafters hung enough championship banners to make a roof on most arenas.

It had been a noisy place in 1924 when it opened to house the Maroons, and in 1996, when the Canadiens scooted to some place named after a phone company instead of classic Rome, the noise remained in the old building and was repurposed along with it two years later.

It took about a year for my guilt about attending bilingual matches in the enemy rink to fall away from my Maple Leaf conscience. I had never seen my boyhood heroes play in Maple Leaf Gardens, after all. I had to settle for seeing them in their blue jerseys trying anything that would make up for the fact that they trailed the Habs in the areas of skating, passing, shooting the puck and so on. I saw Carl Brewer reaching out and trying to grab the jersey of Bobby Rousseau, who had abruptly changed directions and skated away. A few days later Carl Brewer and Bobby Baun were invited by the NHL to quit cutting the palms out of their hockey gloves, which modification made it a little too easy to grasp a *bleu, blanc et rouge* sweater.

Okay, if they could not use their bare hands, there were other parts of the Toronto anatomy to use in an attempt to stop the Frenchmen from Flying. Carl Brewer would play for a different team every year now, but Bobby Baun was still one tough obstacle in front of turncoat Jacques Plante and his many backup goalies in the 1970–71 campaign. Baun knew how to use knees, shoulders, elbows and most other joints to impede a rushing puckhandler in pursuit of his objective. I was there the night he removed the hottest young defenceman in the league from the Montreal lineup.

We are talking about Serge Savard, the first of the big, tall and fast defencemen that changed professional hockey from the days when the average star, forward or blueliner, was about 5-foot-7 and weighed 160 pounds. Savard was 6-foot-3, about 215 pounds, and frightening once he got into top speed on one of the Canadiens' famous rushes up ice. In his first season with the Habs he got his name on the Stanley Cup. In his second season he got his name on the Stanley Cup and became the first defenceman to win the Conn Smythe Trophy as the most valuable player in the NHL playoffs. Anyone with an eye for a dominating hockey player would not be faulted for expecting him to be the best defenceman ever. However, in the 65th game of the 1969–70 season, he sustained an injury that should have ended his career.

He was 23 years old. Among Montreal's defencemen, he was the chief threat to score, and he was the top penalty-killer for the Canadiens. But in that 65th game, he was part of a frantic pileup of Canadiens and Rangers in the Canadiens goalmouth. Vic Hadfield got up. Rogie Vachon got up. Jean Ratelle got up. Bob Nevin, who had just flipped the puck into the unprotected goal, skated away. But Serge Savard did not get up. He was carefully taken away by the medics. Next day in *La Presse* and the *Gazette* we found out that one of Savard's legs had been broken in five places. The bones were being held together by numerous pins. Hockey players are famous for coming back from injuries, even during games, but I remember that we all wondered whether Serge Savard would be able to skate again, much less lift us out of our seats with his famous "spin-o-rama."

I was really glad that I had seen that famous move, especially if it was never going to happen again. The marvellous Canadiens broadcaster Danny Gallivan, who loved to say things such as, "Dryden thrust out his leg in rapier-like fashion and deflected that puck to the corner, where Savard executed his patented spin-o-rama move and sped to the offensive zone," invented that term along with many others. Gallivan was an Irishman from Halifax, where ironic people from a little province loved to use big words. He enriched our hockey lingo in the pre–Don Cherry era.

It is not possible to describe Savard's spin-o-rama, nor is it possible to describe the resultant emotion that would pour through the Forum's crowd as no tiresome "wave" would ever do. After a failed Philadelphia rush, for example, the puck would find its way onto the left-shooting Savard's long stick, and of course there would be a Flyer forward crowding the big defenceman, hoping against hope. But Serge would get his skates under him, lean toward that hapless forward, spin once and drop him behind as he roared with his white-jerseyed companions toward fate at the other end of the ice. When this happened in front of my eyes for the fifth time, I threw away all intentions to continue cheering for those white and blue guys from the Ontario capital, whatever it and they were called.

Of course, Savard missed the rest of that 1969–70 season, and without him the Habs missed the playoffs for the first time in two decades and more. He also missed the first month of the 1970–71 season, but by January he was skating like a tall strong 25-year-old defenceman who did not have hardware holding his leg together. Then on the night of January 30, he came roaring toward the Toronto goal, and got knocked down by Bobby Baun. Savard scrambled to his feet and dealt the Toronto defenceman a not altogether legal riposte, before skating after the puck in the Habitants zone. When he got to the bench, he sat down and could not stand up again. His leg was broken once more.

I saw the Baun hit, and I have to say that it wasn't much of a hit. It certainly did not earn that Savard elbow to the chops. But Serge Savard was out for the season and most of the 1971–72 campaign. It looked as if someone else was going to have to be the best defenceman of the seventies—maybe this Bobby Orr fellow would have staying power. Well, Orr did score a lot of points, and he did make a lot of U.S. dollars, but Serge Savard joined a couple of other pretty good defencemen, Larry Robinson and Guy Lapointe, in winning the Stanley Cup six times in the 1970s. Orr enjoyed that experience twice.

I thought it might be interesting to see what I wrote in my diary the day after that Saturday night when the Savardian spin-o-rama was put out of commission for a year. Apparently, I had been no more impressed than the millions who saw it on *Hockey Night in Canada*. Here is all I wrote: "Last night Hanford Woods and I went to the Forum, where the Maple Leafs beat Mtl 5–4, and it was the best and happiest NHL game I've ever personally seen." So I was still a secret Leafs supporter, even though I had become a Canadiens fan whenever the glorious were playing some other team. Two years earlier I had written in my diary: "I'm in a pretty good mood because I'm just back from the Forum, where I saw Detroit and my two favourite hockey players, Howe and Mahovlich, shut out the Canadiens 4–0. Also saw the big M get a goal, and Ferguson the thug get dumped and penalties, and miss his check. He is, contrary to what I had thought, quite unpopular in that crowd — I was surprised to hear people as well as myself rooting against him. I think that the anglo press, and especially the Vancouver press, have built him up as a Forum favourite. I saw that Bergman is a very good defenceman, and that at least tonight the Detroit defence is very strong, not the worst in the league as they have been called the past few years. Young Unger will be pretty good in a couple years. He was the high scorer in Calgary and London when we were there, but we never saw him."

HANFORD
WOODS

I went to a lot of hockey games with Hanford Woods, and maybe I should spend a little time telling you who he was in those days. But first, a little description of the way he and I and others, such as Ed Pechter and Peter Huse, attended games at the Forum. Today that venue would be called the "iconic" arena in downtown Montreal. In those days we were not so silly. I have to say, though, that we pursued various avenues of silliness, whether we were watching the Canadiens beat the Black Hawks, or watching the Expos lose to the Cardinals.

I did sometimes sit down while watching the Canadiens. In 1970, I bought a ticket for a game against the Vancouver Canucks from a scalper who sold it to me for less than the listed price. Just once I sat high above the east goal, or what Montrealers call the south goal, and marvelled at the way you could see the forwards' passing plays from section 503. I always meant to go to more games up high in the end seats. Sometimes I splurged and bought a six-dollar seat to be beside the aforementioned Hugh Hood and listen to his comical and well-rehearsed shouts.

But usually we occupied standing room, two of us or eight of us, guys in our twenties and thirties who could lean on a barrier for four hours and never lose a point on our wisecracks. At Jarry Park, the French Canadian baseball fans called me "Gypsy," because of my London Bobby's cape and longish hair. At the Forum I used my cape to soften the barrier I was leaning on.

Games started at eight p.m., and the Forum's doors would open at seven. We would arrive some time between 6:30 and 6:45, so we could be the first ones through, usually carrying books to read or preparation for classes. Once there we would race for the escalator on the *rue Lambert-Closse* side, run up the escalator and plunk our coats on the railing behind the TV cameras, behind section 217 or 218. We would watch the teams in their skate-around, and cheer the Zamboni driver as he drove back and forth. If someone had to go for a leak or a cup of coffee, there was nothing to worry about as one guy would be able to watch over four or five coats. Eventually the extra bright television lights would come on, and the red line and blue lines would be as bright as we were. How white the place became, how exciting.

It was too bad that the big TV cameras were in front of us, because they cut down on the number of attendees who got to enjoy our madcap witticisms. We were in the flower of youth; we never got tired of standing there for three and a half hours after a half hour of standing on the sidewalk out front. We were the best minds of our generation, standing and wisecracking in the shrine of North American ice hockey. How ironic that we were leaning and jesting *behind* the CBC/*Radio-Canada* cameras.

I wish we had carried little cameras to those games, so that we would be immortalized in our goofy winter duds. I wish I had made a list somewhere of the names of all of us rail leaners. I remember Hanford Woods and Easy Ed Pechter, and Peter Huse and Dwight Gardiner, but there were several others. Hanford Woods was the only one among us who grew up in Montreal, but he was an exotic just the same. The first time you got a good look at him you decided that he was from a planet a lot like ours but not identical.

Not that he wasn't human-looking. I don't know how tall he was, but he looked kind of tall. He had a long downward nose, and a lot of 1970s hair that frizzed out in an upward direction. I think he wore corduroy pants, or maybe some other brownish cloth, but pants that were baggy anyway, and a big sweater whose sleeves always hung down past his hands, which were kind of long and fingery. He should have been some kind of fifth-century desert capitan with all that flowing clothing. Tall and skinny, he was mostly vertical.

Hanford was one of the few non-Jewish Montreal anglophones that I knew, but like all the Jewish Montrealers I knew, he had an intelligently humorous way of saying things about the world, about literature, music, politics and sports. He was situated as someone outside the status quo, who could have been inside it if he'd wanted to be.

I don't know whether it was true, but I heard that his father was the Dean of Arts at McGill University, so one can understand where he was coming from and how far he wanted to come.

He had in recent years been places far from Montreal. I don't know when he went to university in Buffalo and studied Samuel Beckett under the Beckett scholar and experimental novelist Raymond Federman, but he told me that he left his Beckett thesis on a train or a boat or something, and was too discouraged to start that all up again so decided to go to Jamaica. Good thing, too, because Hanford was the person who introduced this new music called reggae to his cohort in Montreal. He had a lot of vinyl in the age of vinyl, and we were all delighted and thought that Hanford must be a very hip person indeed. In the late sixties and early seventies, Montreal was not as hip as most big cities, partly because so much of its attention was given to the two solitudes and their history or literature, but there was some hipness. For a while one did get to hear musicians such as Albert Ayler and Sun Ra, and I knew of two young poets who had read Jack Spicer and Frank O'Hara.

Of course, Hanford was hipper than most of the Montreal artsy crowd. Between Jamaica and Montreal he had bided for a time in Bolinas, California, the little seaside town just north of San Francisco, populated by poets and musicians, and other people who collectively refuse franchise joints and road signs and new pavement. I mean really famous poets. I believe that when Hanford was first there he would see people such as Robert Creeley and Richard Brautigan every day. Joanne Kyger still lives there, and from what I have been able to find out, Hanford does too, officially, though officially he also teaches literature at Dawson College in Montreal.

Hanford had an amusing and friendly voice that was often used to ask silly or ironic or rhetorical questions. When he really liked something or was impressed as the dickens, he would call it amazing, or really amaaaaaayzing. Nowadays young people say "amazing" the way they say "awesome," to mean sort of interesting. But I knew that when Hanford Woods called something amazing I should maybe pay attention. He was an outfielder on my ball team, the York Street Tigers, and he once called a double play I started "amazing," so I felt as if a Major League scout had given me his recommendation.

Until my last move here in Vancouver, I had a drawing of the Tigers standing and looking into what would have been the camera lens if it had been a team photograph, but I no longer have it. Maybe it went into my fonds at the National Library. Anyway, the guy that looks like the comical guy in a teen TV show is Hanford.

I will give you an idea about how refreshing Hanford Woods's mind is: when he got married to a beautiful woman he had met in Bolinas, and inherited some kids and then helped create another, he persuaded his wife to name the new one Georgia Woods. The last time I saw that girl she was roller skating like mad around the McGill Ghetto, where the Woodses apparently lived when Brian Fawcett and I went looking for them on an occasion I will tell you about later.

Yes, the York Street Tigers were a legend in our time. We played in a two-team league, a doubleheader every

Saturday starting at 11 a.m. in Sainte-Anne-de-Bellevue, against the team sponsored by their company, Domtar, the same Domtar that was laying an inch of soot on my windowsill every day in Westmount. Domtar gave their team a ball field and lots of equipment, and the team responded by winning the pennant year after year. At the end of the week's second game, we would pack ourselves and our fan into my Chevrolet named Arnold and some other car, and head to the pub in Sainte-Anne where we would drink a platelet-replacing lunch.

Anyway, I think it was Hanford who arranged our winter sport. It took me a while to get over my snobbery or work ethic or fear, but eventually, on February 8, 1970, I went to the outdoor rink at McGill University and played my first game with the York Street Seals, a team made up principally of fellows who had a few months earlier been the York Street Tigers. At last this boy from the B.C. desert would play his first hockey game. Some people might call it shinny, and we wouldn't have minded, but our rink had boards and nets, and though we played with galoshes instead of tube skates, and a tennis ball instead of a puck, and though we ignored the ban on icing and offside passes, we didn't get to sit down for a rest often enough, either.

We didn't have Domtar to knock around now, but rather chose up sides, and welcomed some kids to fill the odd empty spot in the lineups. In that first game I wielded my eroded wooden left-shooting stick like a genius at left wing, managing three goals and four assists in our 21–19 loss. (We used volleyball scoring rules.) I also played sensationally during my turn in the net, which was kind of forced on me because I'd fallen and sustained a knee injury.

I remember that Lewis Poteet wore his goofy Barney Google hat from the surplus store in Denver. I wore my bulky red sweater and red toque. That was fine while we were tearing around the ice under the bright sun in the minus-10-degree air. But after the game, when we drove to the *brasserie* for replenishment, it was terrible. We did not have to wear the embarrassing clothes of real hockey players, but as soon as we quit running around, we had bodies coated with sweat inside several layers, including T-shirt covered by sweatshirt covered by prickly sweater. I hated that so much that I nearly quit the Seals. But who could do that? Even after Hanford Woods gave me some separated ribs at the same time that Gordie Howe was enjoying his.

According to my diary, I acquired a new curved wooden stick for my second Sunday at the rink, and was "much improved." And, I wrote, "it's quite an enjoyable sport, though not as deeply informative as softball," whatever that means. I would keep that stick through two seasons on the McGill campus, and though the blade grew a little thinner, it was *my* stick, and when I moved to snowless Vancouver in 1971, I took it with me. For some years it stood in the tall Montreal Canadiens waste can in my office, along with my baseball bat and tennis racket and croquet mallet. Eventually, though, I sawed it a foot shorter and gave it to my little daughter. I don't really remember what she did with it.

I gave her two of my T-shirts, too. One of them had an iron-on Maple Leafs emblem and the other had an iron-on Canadiens emblem. Do you remember those posters we got made from our snapshots in the late sixties and early seventies? We had a poster of our one-and-a-half-year-old daughter Thea wearing one of those T-shirts, which hung from her like a robe. I also have a home-developed photo of me wearing my Toronto Maple Leafs sweater at age 11. I am also wielding a stabber made of an icicle, proof, perhaps, that such a thing could be found in Oliver, B.C., in those bygone years.

Those T-shirts—they fit my infant daughter the way that Hanford Woods's sweaters used to fit him. Looking into my diary recently, I saw more stuff about Hanford and the reviled/adored Canadiens. Further digging provided me with the written-down memory that on October 28, 1970, I had won 90 cents off Ed Pechter by betting on the Leafs, who beat the Canyens 6–2. I was also imagining the gnashing of my brothers' teeth back in Oliver. I recall that Hanford, though a Montreal lad, was not an unironical devotee of the home side. I think that he was really a Boston Bruins follower. In any case, my joy in going to a game with Hanford was partly due to the pageant and colour of the game, and partly due to the outrageous things that Hanford would say while we were there.

"You know, when you really think about it, the Montreal Canadiens are the windmills that Don Quijote attempted to assault."

"Sure, Hanford."

"The independent nation of Equatorial Guinea will be admitted to the National Hockey League as soon as their management fully understands the principle of the free agent."

"Uh huh."

So I had to apply myself diligently to keep up my end

when Hanford was around informing us and the nearby fans of his peculiar slant on hockey and life beyond the rink. Usually I did this by getting louder. I will just tell you about the night of my greatest victory. It had to do with Jerry Korab.

On Saturday night, February 21, 1971, I went to the second Habs game that week along with Hanford Woods, Easy Ed Pechter and Powerful Pierre Huse, this night against the Chicago Black Hawks. Just to keep it interesting, I made a bet with Hanford, he giving me 100 to 1 odds that Jerry Korab, the worst bet I could think of, would get a pair of goals.

The Chicago Black Hawks brought Korab up from the Portland Buckaroos halfway through the 1970–71 season, and told him that his job was to use his intimidating size to keep opposing forwards out of the area in front of the Chicago goal. Korab was big and kind of slow, as hairy as a Philadelphia Flyer, and more or less unknown to the average NHL fan. The Black Hawks, on the other hand, were leading and would win the Western Division. It was a season in which goal-scoring would take a spurt, but Jerry Korab would get only four. He was what they called a "role player." That's a term for a large fellow who can get in the way of your free-skating young scoring star.

So there were four of us leaning on our jackets that night at the Forum. The game turned out to be a laugher, the men in white clearly outplaying the men in red. I don't recall how long ago Korab had been promoted to the big league, and I probably didn't know then. All I noticed was that coach Billy Reay was keeping Jerry Korab on the bench. Come on, I thought to myself, if the Hawks's Hull brothers and Stan Mikita can't compete against Montreal, why not give King Kong a chance? So what if he had not yet scored an NHL goal?

In the middle of the second period I started hollering, "We want Korab!" I guess I had seen his name in the printed lineup.

My three friends joined in: "We want Korab!"

Some of the people in the next row started shouting, "We want Korab!"

"Nous voulons Korab!"

I saw a young guy with a beard, smoking a joint, hollering, "We want Korab, man!"

After the second intermission we were relentless. After every Chicago substitution in the third period, we bellowed louder and louder, "We want Korab!"

Eventually, with the game nearly over and clearly lost, Billy Reay put the big guy out there. We roared our approval. Less than a shift later Korab let go a weak shot from the point that bounced off two Canadiens and eluded Rogie Vachon between the Hab pipes. We became hysterical. It was probably a fortuitous circumstance that our leaning rail was directly behind the *Hockey Night in Canada* cameras. I can still see all the faces turned to look back up at us. Who are these geniuses, their owners were wondering.

After the game a stranger asked me what relation I was to Jerry Korab.

The event reminds me of a night the previous summer, when I was sitting in the left field bleachers at Jarry Park and imploring Bobby Wine to hit a homer there, something he had never done. I shouted encouraging words every time he came to bat, and in his fourth appearance he slapped a liner into the aisle beside me. The Expos fans looked at me with astonished eyes. Bobby Wine did not hit another home run that year.

A few months after Jerry Korab and I had amazed the Forum, the Canadiens beat Chicago in the Stanley Cup Finals. You will remember that in 1971, that battle was between the winners of the Eastern and Western Divisions. Perhaps you will not remember that the Western Division featured a team from Philadelphia, and the Eastern Division was home to the Vancouver Canucks.

I have mentioned that Hanford Woods did a John Ferguson job on me in the rink at McGill. This happened on the second Sunday of January in 1971. Hanford checked me into the boards during our modified-contact game, somehow managing to poke the butt end of his stick high into the right side of my chest. During my illustrious sports career I have had to make quite a few visits to various hospitals due to my experiences on the ice or the grass or the dirt or the floorboards. I moved carefully all Sunday evening, and on Monday morning I betook myself to Montreal General Hospital emergency and waited around for a while, sitting carefully and reading the Montreal newspapers and a good chunk of William Golding's *Pincher Martin*.

Before the afternoon was very old, a young doctor or near-doctor in a doctor outfit touched me here and there and opined that I could have a fractured rib high on the right side in front. He sent me to wait awhile in a chair outside the x-ray room. An hour or so later I was back in my original chair, and he reappeared and told me that the x-rays showed no fracture and no lung damage, so he offered his view that I had some torn cartilage. When I got home to Westmount, I tried to learn to breathe shallowly. Although it was midwinter in Montreal, I tried not to cough or sneeze or even laugh. I phoned my wife, who was on the west coast, where poets did not play ice hockey. She said it was beautiful out there. She didn't know there was a record snowfall coming the next day.

A few nights later she was back in Montreal, and we caught up on things and the next day it was a little more difficult to get out of bed than it had been the day before.

But we tough left wingers want you to know that we play hurt. Our skill level may drop but we are all heart. On Sunday, January 31, we had to spend an hour before the game shovelling snow over the boards, and that is not a recommended activity for forwards with damaged ribs. But all the pain was worth it, as my team beat Hanford's team 26–24.

"You know, when you come to think of it," said Hanford in the overheated bistro after the game, "hockey is a lot like Denmark. There is quite a bit of ice, and no one really reads Kierkegaard."

I looked around the table and saw no great intellectual curiosity about this proposition in the faces of Peter Huse, Bob Holcombe, Jack Klein and Bruce Lorimer. I hoped that each was feeling beads of sweat rolling down the centre of his back inside his itchy sweater. How I envied the professional hockey player who could sit in the dressing room after the game, take off all his embarrassing clothing and hobble into the shower.

Two things happened on February 28, 1971. We found out that Angela was pregnant at last, and I went to my seventh game of the season at the Forum, this time with Hanford Woods, David Cox, my old friend from Calgary days, and Peter and Patty Huse. We got our usual standing and leaning position behind the greys at centre hice, and this time I cheered lustily for Noel Picard (who would get three goals that season), but got only one nearby fan to join us this time, and lost the usual 100 to 1 bet. St. Louis outplayed the Canadiens, but fluked their way to a loss as the locals prevailed 3–2. The Canadiens were winning a lot of games they should have lost, and they would go on to fluke their way past Boston, Minnesota and Chicago on their way to the Stanley Cup, which they skated away with on May 18. A week before that, our two Chihuahuas and I arrived in Vancouver to take up residence in a Kitsilano commune that had included the pregnant Angela for a couple of weeks.

Now reading my diary from that season, I have discovered the moment that I became a true Canadiens follower. On Wednesday, March 31, we had gone to a game that Boston won 6–3, and what a pleasure it was to watch that great Bruins team, the one that should have beaten the Habs in the upcoming first round of the playoffs. Phil Esposito, no matter how much I would learn to dislike him a few years later in Vancouver, was pretty damn impressive, as anyone would be on his way to a 76-goal, 76-assist season. Ken Hodge was going to go over 100 points, too. So would old John Bucyk, whom I had admired when I was a teenager. Bobby Orr was going for 102 assists. (If he had been playing in deflationary 2015, he would have won the scoring championship with 102 points.) Of course he also got 37 goals, which is pretty good for a defenceman. Then there were sub-luminaries such as Wayne Cashman, Johnny McKenzie and Fred Stanfield, each of whom gathered a point a game. Heck, from the guys left over, I could start a pretty good team with Wayne Carleton, Ted Green, Derek Sanderson, Dallas Smith and Ed Westfall.

Oh, and Gerry Cheevers and Eddie Johnston split the goaltending assignments. They let in about two and a half goals a game, pretty darn good in that era.

It had been so much fun watching these guys in black uniforms ploughing into the Canadiens and outscoring them 6–3 on Wednesday night. But on Saturday I cheered very loudly, if you can imagine my doing such a thing, for the home team, and here is why: we were surrounded by avid but unknowledgeable USAmericans from the New York Rangers fan club, big-city yokels in possession of hand-held gas-operated air horns. Oh, how orgasmically enjoyable it was to see the Habs beat the *merde* out of the Blueshirts 7–2! After the game we retired to a tavern for beer and colas: expostulating Hanford Woods, Easy Ed Pechter, the great short story writer Clark Blaise, political scientist David Cox, John Friedman, from whom I had bought rare precious early books by my favourite USAmerican writers, the great short story writer Hugh Hood and I.

I almost missed that game. The night before I had performed in Peter Huse's symphonic piece *Bricolage* in the concert hall at McGill. Avant-garde art is art, I knew, but watching hockey with geniuses is just as important. What a week! Hockey Wednesday. A poetry reading in Ottawa alongside D.G. Jones and John Newlove, my great contemporaries, on Thursday night. The concert on Friday night, and the defeat of the Rangers on Saturday.

In just over a month I would be going to Expos games with Hanford and Clark and Hugh and Ed, sitting in the drizzle and watching the New York Mets go down to defeat.

AUTHORS

You will notice that I seem to connect sports and authors. I used to say that I liked sports because it was something like entertainment whose results you don't know ahead of time (well, unless we are talking about the Toronto Maple Leafs and the playoffs). Most of those guys I went to ball games, hockey games and shinny games with were writers of one sort or another. Even Ed Pechter wrote a terrific crime novel set at the University of California graduate school. It had the sort of wonderful wry title you expect in superior crime fiction: *Publish and Perish*. If I had been a publisher, I would have published it, whether Ed approved or not.

· As you know, there is a lot of baseball fiction, but there isn't much hockey fiction. This may be because people involved in hockey aren't much for reading. The aforementioned Hugh Hood not only attended hockey games and played amateur hockey—he managed to write about it. He wrote *Strength Down Centre,* a nice book about Jean Béliveau. He wrote some neat stories about baseball. He wrote a novel called *A Game of Touch.* But even Hood knew that hockey was made for some other kind of writing. Every pre-Christmas season, all the publishers emit hockey books about every tiny corner of the hockey scene, even the thoughts in a famous rink-redneck's head. But fiction? Not so much, unless you count a stream of kids' books written down to them by non-literary YA producers. On the covers you will see drawings of kids who shoot right.

Clark Blaise's story "I'm Dreaming of Rocket Richard" features a Montreal child with a Boston Bruins sweater, as Roch Carrier's "The Hockey Sweater," the most famous hockey story in the land, features a small town Quebec kid's catastrophic Toronto Maple Leafs sweater, but neither writer wrote a hockey novel. Foster Hewitt's 1949 *He Shoots, He Scores!* begins, "Say, Dad! Detroit Red Wings and Maple Leafs are playing their third Stanley Cup match in Toronto on Saturday night," and ends just after the dad says, "I'm proud of you, Son." So we know what to expect there.

Probably the most successful literary hockey novel in Canada has been Paul Quarrington's *King Leary,* which was published in 1987 by Doubleday, allowed to go out of print and resuscitated in 2008, when fellow writer and musician Dave Bidini nominated it for the CBC's "Canada Reads" book competition. It tells the story of an old-time hockey star who is living in a nursing home, where he is visited by a young advertising huckster who wants to use him in a ginger ale commercial. The story is funny and sad, as Quarrington's novels usually are, and the plot is unlikely, crowded, comical and extravagant, as his plots generally are. Quarrington was a very good fiction writer, and though most hockey fans will never know that, the ones who read books will be thankful that he chose the topic.

His nominator Bidini likes to write about sports, and produced a wry little collection of hockey fictions called *The Five Hole Stories*, published in 2006 by the newish press, Brindle & Glass. Like a lot of the author's writing, the stories are laced with sex and drugs and rude humour. You can be sure that the five holes mentioned are not necessarily those presented to an opposition forward by the defending goalie. One of the stories, though, does involve a notorious female goalkeeper. The book is worth a reading, especially if you need to go and do something while *Coach's Corner* is on TV. Bidini is an amateur hockey player, and his adventures on skates form the basis for much of the writings that he maintains are non-fiction.

Brian Fawcett, who hailed originally from Prince George, B.C., probably does not skate as well as Murray Baron, who was born in Prince George 23 years after Fawcett was, and in a 14-year NHL career with five franchises, accumulated 35 goals and 1309 minutes in penalties. There are many social analysts who will tell you that those stats are to be expected of a Prince George native.

In 2013, Fawcett published a novel about recreational hockey in Prince George and environs. *The Last of the Lumbermen* (Cormorant Books) is narrated by an aging tough guy trying to play through his accumulated injuries and a haze of alcohol mist. This chap, who is smarter than all his teammates, still narrates in small northern-town dialect, a nice old-fashioned humorous realist device.

Twenty-one years earlier, Fawcett published a book called *My Career with the Leafs & Other Stories*. Most of the stories walk the territory that combines autobiography and fiction, stopping to look at back yard hockey rinks, girls at the swimming pool, playing marbles, that sort of thing. But the title story, which comes last in the book, is a departure. Though the style, like that of the other stories, is plain realism, the events in the plot are totally invented, candidly an extended lie, even if the narrator is manifestly other than the author. If Fawcett doesn't mind I will show you what I mean by reprinting the first paragraph here:

> *I'll explain how I came to play hockey for the Toronto Maple Leafs. It was surprisingly easy, and other people with similar ambitions to play in the Big Leagues might be able to pick up some valuable tips. I'm a poet, you see, and one of the things we do as part of our job is an occasional public reading. I had a reading to do in Toronto, and one of the first things I did when I got there was to drop down to Maple Leaf Gardens. The day I went, the Leafs happened to be practicing.*

And so on. They give him a uniform with number 15 on it, and though I am not going to ruin the plot for you, I will say that it involves the relationship between hockey and poetry, which is, you might say, the theme of the book you are now reading. On the cover of Fawcett's book there is a photograph of his son Jesse in full Toronto Maple Leafs uniform and skates, holding a Sher-Wood stick to the ice.

The book came out during the 1982–83 season, and in the spring of 1983, Fawcett was promoting it by reading from it at various venues. Late in March I was doing readings here and there in Ontario, and flew down from Sudbury to meet him in Toronto, where I introduced him to a lot of my poet friends before we took off eastward (as they say there) for joint readings in Kingston and Montreal. I drove his car to Kingston, proceeding at 135 kph except when I had to brake to 100 kph when the radar detector made its sound. So typically Fawcett, I thought, but we got to Kingston in time to have a pleasant evening with Victor Coleman and his students as well as Kingston poets Tom Marshall, David Helwig and Wayne Clifford. I would love to tell you the names of all the poets we had seen in Toronto, but this is primarily a hockey book, not primarily a poet book.

At the reading in an alternate art gallery, Brian wore his Maple Leafs sweater (we hadn't been brainwashed into calling them jerseys yet) with the number 15 on it. We had a lot of fun reading together for the first time, and people told us they thought we had been perfecting this act for ages. Then we had some booze together, and I can say that we had had lots of practice at that. We got in well after two a.m., and the next day was both Easter Friday and April Fool's Day. We celebrated by getting off the highway, driving to Montreal along good old Highway 2. A lot of the towns were new to me as well as to Fawcett— Brockville, Cornwall, Hawkesbury, etc.

Since moving away 12 years earlier, I had been visiting Montreal about once a year, so I still felt a little like a Montrealer, and it was fun to show my younger western writer friend around. He had been there 20 years before, when he was a punk kid, but I had been there as a punk kid too, and a grown writer was going to encounter a different kind of city. When we got into downtown and then to the newly hip *rue St. Denis*, I should have been driving, because the young women were out in their spring outfits, and Fawcett's head was swivelling while he uttered the sophisticated words you would expect from an accomplished literary fellow: "Look at that! Oh, look at that!" That is an unedited quotation.

Brian had Hanford and Susan's address in the McGill Ghetto, so we eventually toodled over there and found his house. The door was open but there didn't appear to be anyone inside, so we just hung for a while. Eventually a beautiful creature came thundering by on roller skates, and as this was back in the day when grown men were allowed to talk to little girls, we made enquiries. It turned out that she was young Georgia Woods, possessor of one of the best names in the Province of Quebec, and yes, she did expect Hanford some time, maybe in an hour. We left a note.

Oh, I still felt like a Montrealer in exile, though I had been an ex-pat longer than I had lived there. On the way "east" through town I showed Brian the apartment building Angela and I had lived in for four years in lower Westmount, where we had resided across the hall from the beautiful short model Jennifer Miles, whose middle-sized dog our Chihuahua Small tried to hump. Now in 1983 she was living across the street from Hanford and Susan, and pretty soon Brian got to meet her, and you know Brian . . . Jennifer was also a friend of Artie Gold, the hotshot young poet who had been my student at Sir George Williams University and who had avidly read my favourite poets.

We were on a literature trip, of course, but there were so many things to do. I had to make contact with poets Lionel Kearns and Michel Beaulieu and other friends. I was also circling closer and closer to a large Riopelle print that I was liking more and more, and which now hangs in my living room. But on Saturday, the night before Easter, there was a game at the Forum against the Boston Bruins.

There were just four of us this time—Hanford and Susan, Brian and I, at a game so popular that we had to buy standing room tickets from a scalper. The place was more packed than I had ever seen it, an estimated 3,500 Bruins fans having bused up to see their bullies take on *les glorieux* at the shrine. Luckily, Hanford had thought of a way to withstand the crush, a bottle of brandy to pass back and forth, thus introducing Brian to another Forum tradition. It was a classic Boston-Montreal game, the Bruins winning 2–1 in the era of high-scoring marksmen.

But here is the reason for recounting this hot spring night. It was April 2, after all, a date that is not known for blistering heat on the Island of Montreal, especially in the evening hours. We were all wearing winter coats, and under his, Brian was wearing his Toronto Maple Leafs jersey with the number 15 and the name FAWCETT on the back. I did my best to reason with him: this is supposed to be a publicity tour for your new book, I pointed out, and how could you better publicize this book than by appearing before the biggest audience in Canada?

He should, I said, make his way down to the boards just as the first or second period is drawing to a close. He should doff his winter coat, and to the shocked dismay of the 17,000 Montrealers and the 3,500 Bruins backers, skate, or rather slide his way out over the ice. Sure, most of the spectators would focus on the fact that he was flaunting the *maudit* Toronto colours, but over the next week the media would be mentioning the Talonbooks hand in all this. Then there was *Hockey Night in Canada*. *Hockey Night in Canada* is to our nation what the Lions and Christians were to ancient Rome, what the corrida is to Spain, what Grand Ole Opry is to the intellectual portions of the USA. I told him that as long as he was not a naked streaker, the CBC and Radio-Québec cameras would stay on him. If he had brought some copies of the book he could throw them into the stands. They might not get thrown back onto the ice.

But oh, no. Fawcett chickened out. To this day he claims moderation, and sometimes he mentions the fact that he probably would have slipped and fallen like a movie comedian of the silent era, thus drawing the wrong sort of attention to his image rather than arousing curiosity about his darned good short story. After the game we discussed the lost opportunity in the Royal Pub, and I didn't get to bed till nearly four a.m.

I don't know how many hockey stories there are among the writings of our literary crowd. We have writers who were or are hockey players but don't write about it, such as Lionel Kearns, Fred Wah, Roy Kiyooka and Paul Dutton. We have writers who were or are hockey players and do write about it, such as Dave Bidini, Grant Lawrence and Robert Kroetsch. There are also some good writers who have never really played hockey, but have written stories and poems and even plays about ice hockey in Canadian life. I am thinking of Diane Schoemperlen's "Hockey Night in Canada," or Rick Salutin's play *Les Canadiens,* or Priscila Uppal's hockey verses in her volume of winter sports poems.

But I do know my favourite hockey story. I liked it so much when I first read it that I included it in a book of sports fiction I edited a couple years later. It was written by the aforesaid Hanford Woods. Not only is it a marvellous story, but it has to be a sure finalist in any contest for best story title: "The Drubbing of Nesterenko."

It was published in Woods's collection, *Two Stories,* by Alithea Press in 1975. The other story in that book is "First Loves," which is also pretty darned good, influenced as it is by its author's favourite writer at the time, Samuel Beckett. The prose resembles modern European writing more than it does any Canadian prose I know. Reading it again almost 40 years after it was published, I find it far more sophisticated than normal Canadian fiction. If Woods were a hockey player he might be a Peter Stastny surrounded by nine John Fergusons. ·

If you happen to be interested in both professional ice hockey and a Euro-like sensibility that has produced writers such as Camus, Genet and Robbe-Grillet, let me direct you toward this hard-to-find story. It is the first-person account of the narrator's arrest and trial for shoplifting records from a department store music section, gathered around a presentation of his fraught relationship with his father, most of which is provided at a playoff hockey game in the Forum. The title refers to a famous hockey incident a few years earlier, in which the Habs and Black Hawks are in a playoff game whose direction is radically altered by John Ferguson's unprovoked clobbering of Eric Nesterenko, a player who was both the opposite of the Montreal mobster, and the narrator's favourite player. A sense of Woods's subtlety can be found in the fact that the one-sided fight resulted in his hating both players equally.

Early we are told of the narrator's "unrelenting hatred of Montreal teams," and I remember that the author, in a seriocomic fashion, used to admit to a similar feeling. Even after I was converted into an admirer of the Habs, Hanford would revile them, even Jean Béliveau, whom he accused of a kind of Québécois Uncle Tomism.

In the story the young student-shoplifter manages to get his trial postponed a few days so that he can attend the first game of this year's series against the "Big Bad Bruins." We are treated to a marvellous minute-by-minute description of what it was like to line up for and race to and endure standing-room spots in the Forum. I felt an acute envy on rereading that scene this time.

I should tell you that I blame John Ferguson and the knuckle-dragging fans who applauded him for bringing about the gradual ruination of the sport I was planning to follow all my life. That is one reason for my appreciation of Woods's description of him, which includes this sentence: "He was hardness itself, a face of rock solid bone, a body of ungainly awkward muscle." We watch with horror and glee while Woods shows Ferguson failing at every skill that hockey requires, except for the brutality that presages the future of the sport.

I used to wonder: could I have been the only person in Montreal who was bothered that the fabulous Flying Frenchmen now looked for their success through the actions of a crude bully from the west coast? Was Canadiens hockey going to suffer this humiliating transformation? Were we to be forced to regard a thug now, without the redemptive palliation of humour?

Once I watched Howie Meeker or some such affable CBC-TV interviewer of limited wit trying to force a clichéd conversation on Eric Nesterenko, who kept pausing and offering a reasoned and intelligent response to his soft-lob questions. Here was this big guy in a funny outfit and sweat pouring off his forehead, making fun of the agreed-upon rules or something. I watched carefully for quite a few years after that, and never again did I see and hear Eric Nesterenko between periods of a hockey game. It took me a while, but I came to understand that *Hockey Night in Canada* was in league with the Fergusons. Eventually they would hire a guy who would put out a series of home videos that reduced ice hockey to a ridiculous montage of goon violence.

Over and over we have seen that if you mention Howie Morenz or even Syl Apps to these gorillas they don't know who you're talking about.

Well, Hanford Woods knows both hockey and thought. He is remarkably accurate about the tactics that are known by the players and missed by most fans. I have never seen such good writing about hockey players and the sport. And I really like this characterizing of our subject: "Hockey is only a game, a stylized activity, a grossly distorted, incomplete miniature of life with all sorts of illusory goals and rewards attached to it."

I believe this to be true still, though Woods wrote those words a while before millions of dollars were being dropped over the heads of lesser-skilled youths.

OFFSHOOTS

I often recall that image of Hanford Woods's daughter on roller skates, loudly travelling the sidewalks below Mount Royal. I wonder whether she ever skated on ice with a bunch of other kids in similar jerseys.

I've known quite a few sons or daughters who became hockey players, sometimes for a while during childhood, sometimes for the rest of their lives, it would seem. I have mentioned Brian Fawcett's son Jesse. He appeared in full ice hockey gear (with the absence of a helmet or face mask) on the cover of his father's *My Career with the Leafs & Other Stories*, but as far as I know, he, like his father, never had any career in hockey. Fawcett's second son, Max, owns a fantasy baseball team in the same league that Brian and I still patronize, but that's about it. He is a magazine journalist in Alberta, where despite those obstacles, he tries to be one of the early arrivals at new trends, and likes to make precise small points in political discussions. In other words, he is just about the opposite of a hockey player.

But I have seen Fawcett's daughter, Hartlea, playing ice hockey, masked and all. Hartlea is a rangy left winger, which, you will remember, was my position. In the game I watched somewhere in a newish sports complex out in Mississauga near Lake Ontario, she pretty well stayed on her wing, offensively and defensively. She seemed to be taller than most of the other 12-year-old girls, to skate faster and react to the puck more quickly. I had heard her father boast humorously that she takes more than her share of penalties, but this day she looked more like a Frank Mahovlich, swift and big. The only thing I didn't see was what old-time hockey scribes liked to call "killer instinct," the thing that can get eager pests past better skaters.

Of course Fawcett was enjoying the game as any ironic softy father should. He was not, I am happy to report, one of those obnoxious but all-too-often encountered hockey parents who excoriate the referees and hurt their own children's feelings. And I wondered: can you say that he was living out his dream through his kid if his kid was not a son? Hartlea's team didn't win, and she didn't get a point, as far as I remember, but I'm glad I was there. If only to see a young girl skate better than I ever could.

Well, I didn't grow up in Ontario, surrounded by indoor skating rinks.

I think you will remember my old friend Lionel Kearns, who grew up in the West Kootenays, surrounded by snow and ice, and who is still playing on a hockey team in his late seventies. His first marriage was to Dolly Maharaj, who was a friend of my girl Joan, with whom I shared that Frank Mahovlich moment I told you about. Dolly was from Trinidad, where ice was something you might encounter in the more expensive tourist hotel bars.

Lionel is a tall Irish-Canadian who once had a thick shag of curly russet hair. Dolly was dark skinned, dark haired and plump, a West Indian whose house smelled nicely of curry. In act II, scene 1 of Shakespeare's *The Tragedy of King Richard the Second*, the title figure is heard to say, "Now for our Irish wars. / We must supplant those rough rug-headed kerns." So naturally, my then-wife, Angela, and my buddy Willy Trump gave the Kearns's first-born son, Frank, the nickname Rughead.

In the early 1970s, young hockey players on the west coast wanted to play at the North Shore Winter Club, a gargantuan sports facility in North Vancouver. That's where I went once with Lionel to watch 12-year-old Rughead Kearns display his skills as a fast-skating centre. His father, I think, had been more of a slow-skating defenceman. Things have changed a lot in the past 40-something years, but at that time it was pretty well a novelty to see a semi-Caribbean boy stickhandling around lads whose unmasked faces were decidedly pale in January. I have lost track of Frank Kearns lately, and I wonder whether he is still playing ice hockey in his early fifties.

In January 1983, I went to Calgary to see artist Judy Chicago's famous show *The Dinner Party* at the wonderful Glenbow Museum, and to perform some poetry at the Off Centre Centre, a terrific alternative art space. I was hosted by D'Arcy Margesson, the great potter and his wife, poet

Vicki Walker. Curiously, they were in our house for a dinner party just this week, more than 30 years later. A few years ago in this house, we made a nearly famous photograph of Fawcett, Margesson, and me sitting together with identical yellow shirts, a uniform of sorts. I am mentioning these things to show how coincidental and complex the life of the arts is when the life of hockey overlaps it.

Anyway, in January 1983, D'Arcy and Vicki took me to see their son Adam play hockey in a new arena on the south side of Calgary. D'Arcy is a tall man with big hands, and Vicki is a spirited redhead from the U.S. prairies. Her mother was a friend of baseball Hall of Famer Harmon Killebrew right there in Minnesota's hockey country. Her oldest child, Adam, was born during the legendary 1972 series between the Soviet and Canadian national ice hockey teams. On this night he was 10 years old, and his team was playing an exhibition game against an older and faster team from another division. Adam's team did not have their regular goalie, so they borrowed a kid from an even more minor division. Nevertheless, I asked Adam to get two assists for me.

Of course they lost 12–2. But Adam impressed me as the best passer on his team, a heady defenceman who didn't give the puck away. It was a pleasure to watch this game played mainly by kids I did not know in a city I had not lived in for the past 17 years. They got the hockey pants knocked off them, but Adam did get me one assist.

Adam grew up to be a marvellous human being, and an amateur hockey player loved by his teammates. He was that combination you wish you would see more often, a straight-A jock. He was his high school class valedictorian, earned a psychology degree at university, married engineering student Jennifer Wu and had a daughter he hoped would be a hockey player. He worked with at-risk kids in Vancouver's east end, and earned a medical degree because he wanted to help the disadvantaged. He was one-eighth Lakota, and particularly interested in the problems of First Nation youth. His mother once wrote a poem that included mention of his pungent hockey equipment.

Then, soon after getting his medical degree he was diagnosed with non-Hodgkin's lymphoma, and died at age 35. At that age, most hockey players are just starting to think about their post-hockey lives.

I have mentioned my lifelong buddy Bill Trump, or "Unca Willy," as he is sometimes known. He was born in the west side Vancouver district that I now live in, and moved with his family to Oliver when he was nine and I was 10. His father Alex, a Brit brought up in China, was athletic in a Brit way; Willy recalls a day when his father stopped the car and jumped into a nearby rugby game that had been short a player. Every once in a while his father's face would show up in a bundle of arms and legs and torsos.

But Bill could not get interested in team sports, as a player or a follower. As a kid he climbed mountains, swam in the lake and zipped around on water skis, but we sort of created the myth that he was uncoordinated. Once at UBC he and his friend Wilson were walking by a table tennis game in process. As they were walking and talking he reached out and nabbed an errant Ping-Pong ball. "Pretty nimble," remarked Wilson, his voice dripping with disappointment.

So, Willy has often wondered, did his daughter Monica inherit her sports agility from the grandfather she didn't know? As a little girl she joined in every game that was going, and when there was no game going she would invent a game that involved running around cars and leaping over fences. The only sport that her father ever invented was "economical ball," and he shared the credit with his buddy George. In economical ball there weren't any teams. About six of us kids would sit in a circle on chairs in Bill's basement. There would be some ball, maybe a volleyball or soccer ball, and a player would gently kick it or bat it with a broom or push it with a hand toward another player. The object was to expend as little energy as possible while never rising from one's chair. We were a gang of 11-year-old ironists.

But Monica! She was a goalie in high school floor hockey, but she hadn't skated much. So when she joined an ice hockey team she did not know how to skate backward, and the only way she could stop was by skating into the boards. She never got any advice from her mother Akiko, who was from Japan and not inclined toward Canadian contact sports. She was a long way from Canadian artist and poet Roy Kiyooka, who had played rover on prairie hockey teams made up mostly of Ukrainian-Canadian skaters twice his size.

Monica applied herself, as she did to all facets of her life, and got better and better as her rookie season went on. I decided that I wanted to attend one of her games in Kitsilano with her father. By this time Willy could not see all that well. From his uncles he had inherited the family genetic disease, retinitis pigmentosa, a progressive condition that starts with bad night vision, becomes tunnel vision and often proceeds to complete blindness. Willy has been legally blind for years. But when I went to that hockey game with him he could still see some. He just couldn't see halfway across the rink.

So as with other things, I was there to describe things for him. In the previous summer, for example, I had described the women's swimsuits at Kits Beach. He is my lifelong friend, and I will do just about anything for him.

"She's down again," I said on this occasion.

Willy pointed his face in the general direction of the play.

"She's up," I said. "Oh, she almost received a pass."

Willy had never been much interested in professional hockey, so I stayed clear of the game's technical language.

"She's down again," I said.

But Monica got better and better, until each year she was the best player on her team, and often had to step up and play on a team of older girls. Eventually she would become the oldest player on her team. In recent years she has often been recruited to fill a spot for a team of women half her age that finds itself a few women short for an important game. From what I hear (well, from Willy) she is still the best player on any team she winds up on.

As an adult, Monica did not, as far as I know, play the two team sports you might expect of women—softball and basketball. What was her other team sport? Football. No, not soccer.

My daughter has never been into ice hockey. She did some figure skating, as a lot of girls growing up in Kerrisdale did. But being her father's kid, she also played some softball. Being her father's kid, she knew the rules a lot better than the other girls did. She's left-handed, and has a blue baseball glove, and still gets to play some ball in Edmonton. Not enough, though.

My sister's three daughters never played hockey, though one of them left the desert valley to spend her adult life in southern Alberta. My daughter has 10 cousins, nine of them girls, none of them hockey players. But things have changed in the South Okanagan valley. No longer do kids from the prairies have to hike up into the hills and clear snow off ponds to get in some ice hockey. There's an indoor rink in Oliver. There's another one in Osoyoos. There's television galore, so kids can see how the pros do it. There's a whole world of kids' activities organized by grown-ups. A teen playing hockey now does it with a word on his chest, often a name that has nothing to do with the place in which he lives.

Somewhere in the lower Fraser Valley there was a professional ice hockey team called the Heat. Apparently the name won first place in a name-the-team contest. I imagine that the Humidity came second and the Smog came third. Hey, thought management, Heat—what a good name for a winter game played on ice! A team in the southeast of B.C. is called the Ice. No imagination, eh? Now there is a Junior B team in Chase, B.C. It's kind of cold in hockey season up there, but it says "Heat" on their chests.

So now, in my valley, where we played baseball from April till October and basketball from November till March, parents have the privilege of forking out hundreds and hundreds of dollars for equipment so they can outfit their sons for practice at six a.m. I haven't heard of any girls' teams there, though I have heard the kids offering up their poor opinions of gay people; so I rather imagine that the *Coach's Corner* culture prevails.

Neither of my brothers had any children that got into playing hockey, though one of my twin nieces is crazy about the Montreal Canadiens, and phones home from West Kelowna every time the Habs score a goal on TV. She even made her way to Montreal one time, and swooned below the statue of Guy Lafleur in front of the Bell Centre. Along with her sisters, she gave her children misspelled and made-up names. In that way they carried on the work of their great-grandfather's family, who came to Canada from the Ozarks. So Emmette and Ephriam and Virgal were followed by a couple generations of Frank and Sally and James, then honoured by a generation that included Saira, Angellique, Brenden and Jaymin.

According to my brother, Jaymin's grandfather, the boy is a hockey wunderkind. His last name isn't Bowering, though. It's Dias. Last I heard, his Midget tier three team won a championship. I saw a picture of the pennant they won. It says "Omaha" on it. Maybe I will get around to explaining that in my last chapters.

The only Bowering hockey player I ever heard of was apparently no great shakes. Years and years ago I was doing a spring reading in Regina, and as I always do, I bought a copy of the local newspaper, in this case the *Leader-Post*, one of the Canadian newspapers that had book reviews in it back in the day. I turned to the sports pages, and found that the Regina Pats juniors had a defenceman named Bowering. I don't remember his first name, but I do remember that almost at the end of the regular season he had two points, both assists. I figured he must be what the hockey people call a "role player."

SPEAKING
of NAMES

Nowadays you don't see very many nifty names in hockey. All the players now are named Ryan or Drew or Colton. But back in the day we kids in the front room listening to the radio recited with wonder the names of Bep Guidolin and Teeder Kennedy.

So I have given some thought to drafting my own fantasy team, based on names. I'm not including Finnish names, etc., because a lot of them sound pretty funny to start with. My first string would look something like this:

Bep Guidolin   Metro Prystai   Boom-Boom Geoffrion

Sheldon Kannegiesser   Bucko McDonald

Turk Broda

My second unit would consist of:

Pete Babando   Newsy Lalonde   Eddie Shack

Dit Clapper   Jeff Beukeboom

Gump Worsley

—and so on. I would find a way to get ice time for Toe Blake and Muzz Patrick, Butch Goring and Busher Jackson, Orland Kurtenbach and Bun Cook. I have a notebook full of names to round out my roster and supply my American League affiliate. Yikes! I forgot Mud Bruneteau, my childhood hero.

Here's one thing I found out while drafting this squad: for some reason the position of left wing gets the highest number of neat names, whether we are talking nicknames or given names. Come to think of it, you could line up a team of nicknames (Pocket Rocket Richard, etc.) against a team of given names (Wally and Nip Hergesheimer, etc.). All this makes a fellow wish that Rob Klinkhammer had played more than one game with the Blackhawks, or Fred Saskamoose more than 11.

Did you ever think of selecting a team on the basis of weather? You would, of course, start with Cyclone Taylor, the city of Vancouver's best player of all time. He was a defenceman back east before he came to the coast and operated as a centre for the lucky Millionaires, whom he led to Vancouver's first, and probably last, Stanley Cup victory in 1915. Nowadays there is a hockey rink and a chain of sports equipment stores named after him.

You would raid the Maple Leafs wartime roster for Windy O'Neill, and if you are a fan of early season climate you'll sign Terry Crisp, and put him on a line with Harry Frost and Patrick Sharp. Garth Snow would have to be your goalie. In 2007–08 there was a 34-year-old defenceman, Quinn Fair, who played parts of three games with the Bakersfield Condors of the East Coast Hockey League. As for really rounding out the player list? You could talk trade with the Tampa Bay Lightning or ask the Wichita Thunder about some prospects.

The animal kingdom might supply a clearheaded general manager with a team of something wilder than oxen. Moose Vasko and Moose Dupont would, of course, anchor the defence. They might also serve as bodyguards for Bunny Larocque. Bennett Wolf could play some dogged defence for your zoo as long as you can keep him away from Joe and Mark Lamb. You'd better watch Tiger Williams, too. Maybe the Penguins defenceman Chris Tamer could be your coach.

Well, as you can imagine, I could do this all day. But I have a book to write. Why don't you take a (short) break from reading and make up a team from the names of body parts, Toe Blake, of course, and Dick Duff, etc. You could go for tools, such as Troy Mallette and his little brother Dave "The Hammer" Schultz. You could hire a bunch of skating tradesmen, starting with Bill Barber and King Clancy. Things to eat? Items of clothing? Words you can't say with a mouthful of cake? (I'm thinking Ezinicki for a start.) You get the idea. Now let me get back to work.

LEAVING *the* CAPITAL
CITY *of* HOCKEY

My four years in Montreal were eventful, not just because the Canadiens were so exciting. We lived there from 1967 to 1971, which means that while we were living there the Métro, Montreal's quiet rubber-tired subway system, observed its first birthday and delivered millions of people to the last great World's Fair, Expo '67, Man and His World. In 1969, Major League Baseball arrived in the form of the brightly dressed Expos, who cavorted in the all-aluminum Parc Jarry, where the Cardinals and Dodgers came to play before the snow had melted from the warning track, and one day a wooden miniature baseball bat was given to every kid who came to the game, resulting in the biggest noise in the city until the FLQ Crisis. The FLQ Crisis occurred just after the Expos' second summer, when separatist terrorist cells kidnapped the British trade commissioner and a Quebec cabinet minister.

For a few years we had been getting used to FLQ bombs in mailboxes and the like, but now with the kidnapping of politicians and the subsequent murder of Pierre Laporte, the Canadian government invoked the War Measures Act and over 450 people were imprisoned without charge. French-language poetry books and music albums were removed from stores, and 18-year-old soldiers with rifles guarded the doors of the Forum, even though everyone knew that no Québécois would ever drop a bomb on the Habs ice.

I felt really awake in those times. I did not have to hop on a bus for Selma or Chicago to keep my eyes open. In January 1969, we had our own crisis at Sir George Williams University, where I was first the writer-in-residence and later a professor of English. The trouble started when some Caribbean students accused a professor of racism and occupied the ninth-floor computer lab. Soon 450 students, black and white, joined in the occupation, and a lot of us younger faculty made our demands on the intransigent administration. Business students stood in the street around the Hall Building, and when they saw black faces at the ninth-floor windows, they shouted, "Jump! Jump! Jump!" Eventually there was a riot, and some damage was caused to the computers, either by students or riot police. There were 100 arrests, most of the charges later dropped. Among the occupiers were one future prime minister (Dominica) and one senator (Canada).

So you see, I was living in Montreal during an interesting time, and not just because Guy Lafleur finally removed his helmet and got the fans who had been booing him to turn around and make him their new hero in flying locks.

But I won a Canada Council grant to take time off work and write a novel, and decided to write it in Vancouver. We closed up our long apartment, entrusted our books and scant furniture to a moving van and prepared to leave the land of snow. It was also the land of air pollution, which led me to apply for a job at Simon Fraser University. Just as I had done when I left the University of Calgary, I used a grant to start an ambiguous transition. We hoped that we were moving back to the coast, but there was a chance that we would return to Habs country. I did feel bad that just when I was finally living in a city with a Major League ball team, it looked as if I might be moving back to minor league country. You might say the same thing regarding hockey, considering the ability of the Vancouver Canucks.

Anyway, Angela, who was pregnant at the time, got onto a Boeing 747 and flew to Vancouver, where she would take up residence in an urban commune (this was the early seventies, remember) in the same neighbourhood in which we had lived before we left town in 1963. I would get myself, my typewriter and our two Chihuahua dogs into my Chevrolet and drive across the country to join Angela and our five friends in a bungalow in Kitsilano, there to write my book and await word on whether I would be going back to work at Sir George or Simon Fraser.

Did I zoom! The dogs, who had gone back and forth across the continent by car a few times, were nice and quiet in every motel I snuck them into, and slept while I managed up to 700 miles a day in my underpowered six-year-old Bel

Air. We spent one night in Moose Jaw after I had started hallucinating during a dark and complicated bypassing of Regina. There just before midnight I wrote in my diary:

> I noticed one night in Montreal last week that it was easy to drive around because there was a Canadiens playoff game on TV and radio, and the streets were nearly deserted. Tonight I was driving across Saskatchewan while the first game of the final series was on, and there was all at once nearly no traffic on the TransCanada Highway. I decided to drive till the game was over, but it went into a second overtime period, and I couldn't make it. I stopped after the first overtime period for food, and now I don't yet know who won. I got blear-eyed, and driving in the dark, I got lost in a maze of lights and roads while trying to bypass Regina. I had to drive around and try again, so I wound up driving 750 miles again today.

I guess it was a good thing that so many potential drivers were at home watching the game. By the way, the Chicago Black Hawks beat the Canadiens 2–1 in that game, but never fear, the Canadiens would win the series in seven games.

What an interesting way to follow the Stanley Cup playoffs! I'll bet that a lot of people have done it. The next night I managed 650 miles with no game to listen to, and stayed over in Creston. I had stopped in Irvine, Alberta, for a rotten cup of coffee, and had a chat with the trucker guy who was driving our furniture to Vancouver. Three times I passed the same little Renault with Québec plates, and exchanged waves with the two young women in it. I wondered whether they were Danny Gallivan listeners.

The dogs and I got to Oliver, my home town, in time to watch game 2, which Chicago won 5–3, and I walked carefully, because my father had been a Habs fan since before I was born, and my two kid brothers, 25 and 22 years old, were in the not-so-early portion of their lifelong devotion to the Canyens. I will admit that I was leaning in that direction a little, perhaps mainly because Montreal was a more-or-less Canadian city.

The Chihuahuas had been born in Oliver seven years earlier, and they now enjoyed the warmest spring in their lives. I was digging it too, this rural life so far away from the centres of poetry and significant Canadian life. I did not mind when my parents beat me at golf on their arid course, or when I lost a dime to my dad on the Washington-Minnesota baseball game. I couldn't help noticing how nice it was not to taste bad-flavoured chemicals in the air. On Saturday, May 8, an off-day for the playoffs, I got an unexpected treat. I looked out my parents' front window and saw my old friend Mike Matthews, who was known as "Magic Mitt" because of the trouble he had with foul pop-ups while playing third base on the York Street Tigers a couple years ago in Montreal. He had been to a community college conference in Kelowna and missed the Vancouver turnoff on his way back home. We had hamburgers and played a game of catch, and off he went. The dogs, Frank and Small, were really glad to see him.

And next day? We watched an afternoon game in which the Habs went down 2–0 before Frank Mahovlich led them to a wonderful comeback win, 4–2. During the game I wore my T-shirt with the Canadiens logo on it. What a wonderful way to bond with my dad: he got to see his beloved Canadiens finally win a game, and I got to see my old hero Frank Mahovlich save the redshirts in the game that could have destroyed their hope. All this inside on a bright hot Sunday South Okanagan midday.

On Tuesday, the Canadiens won an easier one to tie the series, and the next day Frank and Small and I were at the commune on York Avenue in Vancouver. As luck would have it, our furniture beat me there, and our little TV set would become a centre of attention for a few hours on the 13th (Chicago 2, Montreal 0) and the 16th (Montreal 4, Chicago 3). Then on Tuesday night, May 18, 1971, we communards gathered around that little colour TV and watched a hockey game that a lot of people justifiably remember as the most exciting game seven in Stanley Cup history.

Montreal, everyone agreed, should not have been playing hockey this late in the year. They had finished third in the Eastern Division, 24 points behind the Boston Bruins. Then, because of the odd new playoff structure, they met the Bruins in the first round and won the series 4–3. For three years running, the East had been demolishing the West because the first two rounds had been confined to divisional games. First, the expansion Vancouver Canucks had been placed in the Eastern Division, and the Chicago Black Hawks had been moved to the West. Then the opening round saw divisional games between first- and third-place finishers and second- and fourth-place finishers.

It so happened that the Minnesota North Stars lost their last four games to fall into fourth place by one point so that they would not face the powerful Hawks in round one. A lot of people had a sneaking suspicion that the North Stars could have done better, let's say. Are you with me? The next stage of looniness had the 1–3 winner in the East play the 2–4 winner in the West. And *vice versa*.

So the Canadiens, who had pulled off an upset to win their first round, had pushovers for their second round. But the North Stars, who had had so much trouble in their last four games of the regular season, sucked it up and pushed the Canadiens to six games in round two. Well, said everyone, that was an exciting postseason, but now the Chicago Black Hawks, who played a tough semi-final including three overtime games against the Rangers, were ready with their home-ice advantage to halt the Montreal dream.

But wait, said the dreamers. The Black Hawks were the best in the West, which had given them a record just below New York's, and only 10 points better than Montreal's. But, hey, they were the Chicago Black Hawks. They had Bobby Hull and Dennis Hull, Stan Mikita and Pit Martin and Tony Esposito. And what about this? The Canadiens had knocked off the Bruins, who had set scoring records this season because of Phil Esposito and Bobby Orr. And here we were on Tuesday night, with the series knotted at three, and Jean Béliveau suited up for the last game in his beautiful career.

But there was this: Chicago Stadium was the biggest, noisiest, smelliest arena in hockey. There were lots of fistfights in the upper regions, and blood on the floor to more than equal the blood on the ice. In Tom Clark's poem "Chicago" (from *At Malibu*, New York, Kulchur Foundation), he remembers working in that huge barn as a teenager:

> Third Balcony at the Chicago Stadium defies
>   fantasy.
> Its denizens are capable of every heinous act.
> Stabbings, even abortions, take place during hockey
>   games.
>
> Blackhawk fans hurl pennies and eggs onto the ice.
> The pennies and eggs immediately freeze over,
> Leaving small bumps on which it is hoped
>
> Opposing players will skate, tripping dangerously.
> But hockey fans are angels compared to the folks
> Who show up for boxing. At the Robinson-Fullmer
>   fight
>
>   (May Day 1957)
>
> I'm working in the Third Balcony. Fights, of course,
> Erupt bloodily all around me; it's not my job
> To interfere, only to report deaths & serious
>   woundings
>
> [etc]

There had been seven game 7s in the Stanley Cup Finals, and the last one had been in 1965, when the Canadiens shut out the Hawks 4–0. There would not be another one until 1987. This 1971 one between Montreal and Chicago would be the last one contested by two pre-expansion clubs. No visiting team had won a game 7 since the 1945 Toronto Maple Leafs barely knocked off the Red Wings, and it would not happen again until 2009, when Pittsburgh beat the Red Wings at the Joe Louis Arena.

Yes, the Canadiens were the underdogs. That situation was grudgingly admitted by the trinity of TV announcers on CBC's *Hockey Night in Canada*—Ward Cornell, the Worselyish studio host; the great play-by-play man, Danny Gallivan; and colour commentator Dick Irvin, Jr. That opinion was unanimously held at CBS, who would have the largest USA television audience ever for an NHL game. So the best playoff game ever was watched by the most people ever. As a matter of fact, you can still watch it, or at least the best parts of it, by employing your computer search engine of choice.

Once the game started, in front of the snarling, bleeding fans at the Stadium and the crowd of Vancouverites in the living room on York Avenue, it looked as if the pundits in Las Vegas were right, and the Habs had fought heroically, only to fall a game short.

Maybe the Dryden story was finished. In one of the most famous risks in NHL history, coach Al MacNeil had benched goalie Rogie Vachon and replaced him with a tall quiet guy named Ken Dryden, an Ivy Leaguer, of all things, for the playoffs. Dryden had been one of those stories the newspapers and broadcasters play for, as he shut down Esposito and Orr to start with, and then hauled the Habs past Minnesota and into game 7 in Chicago. But here it was, late in the second period, and Dryden had allowed two goals, while Tony Esposito, a one-time Hab, was working on a shutout. Even the Mahovlich brothers, who were to set new scoring records in this series, could not manage to dent the Chicago goal. Then Bobby Hull banged his famous slapshot off the crossbar, and Dryden looked a little dazed, even inside his skinny goalie's mask.

Did Jacques Lemaire, who was the proprietor of one of the game's best slapshots himself, know that Esposito was supposed to have trouble keeping his eye on long shots? Maybe he was just acting out of frustration when he set the puck up at the centre red line and flailed away at it. The 18,400 witnesses were relaxed in a murderous way. The puck suddenly dipped and passed under Esposito's catching hand, and the Canadiens were on the scoreboard.

Before the period ended, Henri Richard scored the tying goal, and right after the third period started, the Pocket Rocket scored the go-ahead goal. Having seen him fly up the ice and score with his quick right-hand shot many times, I found no trouble enjoying his red-sweatered blur on this occasion as I noisily watched the game from the west coast. I always loved Henri Richard. Did you know that he got 81 more points than did his brother Maurice? I wish I had seen the Rocket live, but I am so glad that I got to watch Henri lead the famous headman rush. I wish that Claude Richard, who was called the Vest Pocket Rocket, though he was a little bigger than Henri, had made the team.

Oh, and did I mention that Henri Richard stood 5-foot-7 and weighed 155 pounds?

But where were we? Oh, yes, period three. After Richard's goal the Black Hawks came on like the Gods after the Titans, and the Canadiens fought furiously to make it through the last 17 minutes and 26 seconds, while Ken Dryden kept making saves that would break a mother's heart if that mother were Mrs. Hull or Mrs. Mikita. When it was over all the players skated in two ragged lines to shake the customary hands, then somehow made it to their dressing rooms to collapse on benches and floors.

ALL *the* BROTHERS
WERE VALIANT

One of the wonderful things about the Richard brothers was that they played all their major league games for the same team. In fact, before Henri came up to the NHL Canadiens, he played for the Montreal Junior Royals, the Montreal Royals and the Montreal Junior Canadiens. Henri wound up running a tavern, and for years after moving back to the west coast, I kept a paper placemat from that place. It was really corny, but I prized it as a souvenir of centre-ice greatness. I gave it to my own brother Roger for his Habs collection. I also gave him my oversized Henri Richard lapel button, etc. Maurice Richard supplemented his old-age pension by tying fishing flies in his basement and selling them to sporting goods stores.

The Richards gathered 902 goals and 2,011 points between them. You should remember that back when

Maurice was in his prime, and Henri was starting out, it was not common practice for scorekeepers to hand out two assists on every goal they could. I wish that Maurice had been, say, 14 years younger, so that the Richard brothers and the Mahovlich brothers could have played for the Habs at the same time. As you know, the "Big M" was my favourite player, and his younger brother pleased me pretty well, too. He was called the "Little M," though he was five inches taller and five pounds heavier than Frank.

The Mahovliches weighed 75 pounds more than the Richards, and they were 12 inches taller, but although they were both pretty exciting hockey players, they did not do as much damage to opponents' cages as the Rockets did. Frank and Pete got 821 goals between them, 890 if you count Frank's goals for the Toronto Toros and Birmingham Bulls in the WHA. They amassed 1,876 points, or 2,108, if you count Frank's WHA helpers.

As you know, Frank became my travel agent when I did a reading tour of the Northwest Territories, and later still he was a Canadian senator while I was the Parliamentary Poet Laureate. As for Peter: he has taken the more usual post-career path, having coached and scouted for a lot of different teams in a lot of leagues.

I guess the big competition for the Mahovliches in the brother business was provided by the Hull brothers. Dennis Hull, who was the Peter Mahovlich of the Hull brothers, never got a nickname, even though his brother was "The Golden Jet." Why couldn't he have been "The Cement Jet" in honour of the main industry of the Hulls' birthplace, Point Anne, Ontario? Maybe the Chicago sportswriters have a thing against nicknames. All they could do for Michael Jordan was "MJ," or "Air Jordan," and the great Ernie Banks had to settle for his name. Yes, I know about Three Finger Brown, but that was back in the age of steam, and as for "The Big Hurt"? He played for the White Sox. The White Sox don't count.

They used to say that for a goaltender the scariest thing to see was Bobby Hull's stick getting ready for a slapshot. Later in his career it would be the sight of his hair implants after two periods of play. It is often opined that hockey goalies must be mentally unhinged as a condition of getting between the pipes, and who could doubt it upon seeing Gerry Cheevers or Roger Crozier suit up to play the Chicago Black Hawks and their left winger? Bobby got 610 goals in an NHL career that lasted only until he was 33 years old, and when he left for the WHA, he was the second-highest scorer in NHL history. Then he went and got 303 more goals in the WHA! Let's say that his goal total was 913, and his points total was 1,808. Now what about Dennis? His career was shorter than his brother's, but he managed 303 NHL goals and 654 points.

So the Hulls got 1,216 goals and 2,462 points. That beat the Richard brothers handily and the Mahovlich brothers by a lot. They almost beat the Gretzky brothers.

But wait! We're not finished with Hulls. Bobby Hull has a son who was called "The Golden Brett" by a generation of sportswriters who were easily satisfied when it came to inventing nicknames. No one knows how many of them were tempted to type "The Golden Bratt." Brett Hull's parents showed the same level of inventiveness, naming their sons Bobby, Brett, Bart and Blake. At least they called their daughter Michelle, not Brianna.

Brett grew up a rich kid in Illinois and Manitoba, until his mother couldn't stand the latter anymore. Brett went with her to North Vancouver when she left Bobby Sr. He'd been a really spectacular offensive hockey player all during his childhood, but when he got old enough to play junior hockey, he made no impression on the NHL draft; the tier-one Canadian Hockey League is a developmental league, after all, and it didn't look as if the overweight rich kid was going to develop much. So he went to Penticton. It had been a long time since I'd seen bloodthirsty senior hockey there, but now there was a tier-two organization called the B.C. Junior Hockey League, and the Penticton Knights were in the Interior Division. Brett Hull went there and started scaring the bejesus out of 17-year-old goalies. He could not skate as well as his mother, but during his two years as a Knight he used the family slap-shot and other innate skills to rack up 153 goals and almost as many assists in 107 games.

The Calgary Flames said ah, what the heck, and picked him 117th in the 1984 entry draft. But he accepted an invitation to college in the U.S. instead, where for two years he drove fear into the hearts of scholar goalies as the first-line right winger of the University of Minnesota-Duluth. As he had done in Penticton, he set a lot of team records in Duluth. So the Flames persuaded him to abandon his studies, and sent him for a year to their Moncton team in the American Hockey League. For the conveniently named Golden Flames he set more scoring records, and in 1987 he became a full-time Calgary Flame, until March 1988, when he was traded to the St. Louis Blues.

The Blues were pleased with him despite the usual

concerns about mediocre skating, imperfect conditioning and a seeming unconcern for defensive hockey playing. Hull took over as St. Louis's top scorer, and started a career as hockey's most famous out-of-shape hockey star. As every hockey fan knows, he played for Calgary, St. Louis, Dallas, Detroit and Phoenix. He got to one more team than Wayne Gretzky's NHL total, and was the biggest scoring star in the league following "The Great One."

So what have I been getting at? Well, in his NHL career (admittedly all in the post-expansion era) The Brett beat all The Jet's NHL records. But perhaps more important, the Hull family wound up with 1,957 goals and 3,853 points. Take that, Wayne Gretzky!

But the first NHL brother act I knew of was made up of Nick Metz and Don Metz. How neat, I thought years later when the Canadian army had a NATO base in Metz, France. I knew the nifty names of these two men because Foster Hewitt used to say them along with the name of Wally Stanowski while I was listening to *Hockey Night in Canada* and doing my math homework. You will remember that I told you about my dream of their Maple Leaf team in the forties. You might say that they were the anti-Hulls, given that though Don might have played on five Stanley Cup teams and Nick on four, they amassed only 151 goals between them, and 305 points.

I suppose that during my really early years as a hockey fan, the most famous brother act had to be the Bentleys, Max and Doug. I was so excited to hear about them— especially after Max came to Toronto in a famous five-for-one deal that didn't turn out all that well for the Black

Hawks—that to this day I remember that they were from Delisle, Saskatchewan. Once, when I was pretty well middle-aged, I was driving from Edmonton to Winnipeg for some reason, and while I was tooling by Saskatoon, I went off Highway 16 just to drive down the short main streets of two little towns, Delisle and Floral, the home of Gordie Howe. I don't know why I have remembered these towns all my life. Sakatchewan is the only province west of the Maritimes that I have not lived in. They were neat little towns, threadbare in their post-railroad condition. I'll bet the kids are out skating pretty early in the winter.

In the thirties there were six Bentley brothers and seven Bentley sisters skating in Delisle, where their dad was the mayor and saw to the building of the Delisle Arena. In the middle of the Second World War, the NHL rosters were looking for decent players, and for 11 games in the 1942–43 season, Reg Bentley joined Max and Doug on a line for the Chicago Black Hawks. He got one goal, assisted by his brothers, then spent the rest of his long career in the minors. His two more-famous brothers, playing during a time when the schedule called for 50 games, accounted for 462 goals and 1,075 points.

By the way, Max was the heaviest Bentley at 155 pounds. Doug weighed 145.

Also, by the way, Gordie Howe did not get to play alongside his brothers, though there were a lot of them. Vic Howe scored three goals for the New York Rangers in the fifties. But Gordie's sons Mark and Marty played alongside him in the WHA and the NHL, and Mark, a two-way defenceman, would have reached the Hall of Fame if he had been the son of Clem Kadiddlehopper.

Well, there were a lot of family acts. There was a time when the name Conacher pretty well *meant* hockey. In the late twentieth century there were about 50 or 60 Sutters playing and managing in pro hockey. My boyhood hero Syl Apps (I used to enjoy walking around and saying his name out loud—try it) was the Leafs captain, and the father of Syl Apps Junior, who got 99 points for the Pittsburgh Penguins in 1975–76. Syl Jr.'s daughter Gillian Apps has been one of the best women's hockey players in the world, having been on teams that won a lot of world and Olympic championships.

One of the few women players who has exceeded her has been Hayley Wickenheiser, cousin of Doug Wickenheiser, who played in the NHL. She exceeded him, too. Doug spent his first big-league years with the Canadiens, generally skating between the boos he was offered from both sides of the rink. The Montreal fans and sportswriters didn't like him at all, for two reasons. 1. He had a non-French name and came from Saskatchewan instead of Quebec, and the Montreal management drafted him instead of Denis Savard, who went on to be a super-star for some other team. 2. He wasn't all that good as a skater and playmaker, and he was no sniper. Of all the hockey brothers, the Molson brothers have often been among the least popular in the province of Quebec.

Doug Wickenheiser's cousin Hayley started the way any future superstar is supposed to. She got born in a tiny Saskatchewan town, Shaunavon, put on skates just after she learned to walk, and headed for the nearest outdoor rink. She grew to be taller and heavier than any Bentley, and wound up being the best woman hockey player in the world. She played pro hockey (men's) in Finland, and led the Canadian national team (women's) to championship after championship. She was responsible for making male TV hockey fans turn on the secondary sports channels where her team could be seen outskating the European and American opposition.

Okay, we have seen brothers and fathers and daughters and cousins. The NHL is that kind of place. The DiMaggios were pretty good in baseball. The father-and-sons act called the Mannings is a kind of cracker royalty in the National Football League. Two giant Ukrainian brothers recently owned all the heavyweight boxing crowns. In the National Basketball Association we have the Spanish brothers Pau and Marc Gasol, and the seven-foot identical twins Brook and Robin Lopez.

Spanish? Well, in hockey, the word for Spanish is Russian. At the end of the twentieth century we got to see Pavel Bure, a great two-way hockey player, and his kid brother Valeri Bure, a very good hockey player who now grows wine grapes in California. That makes some kind of sense, because there is a wine-growing area in Switzerland near the French border, where the municipality of Bure lies. But isn't Switzerland better known for watchmaking than wine-growing? The great grandfather of Pavel and Valeri Bure was a Swiss watchmaker who was summoned by Tsar Alexander III to make his watches. The Bures kept making watches for the tsars for a hundred years until there were no more tsars.

Watchmakers are not vintners, and the Bure family was from a place called Furna, which is as far from Bure as you can get and still be in Switzerland. Still, if you look at the labels on Valeri Bure's wines you might see a little watch and a little hockey stick.

Twins? Consider the Lamoureux twins of Grand Forks, North Dakota. Their father, Pierre, crossed the border into the U.S. northern Midwest, as French-Canadians have been doing for a couple hundred years, played backup goalie at University of North Dakota, married a blonde athlete and produced six hockey offspring, two of them being Monique and Jocelyne, who were born July 3, 1989. They went to university, first Minnesota, then North Dakota, and finished as the two highest scorers in the Western Collegiate Hockey Association. They have also been playing for the U.S. national team, sometimes edging, more often being edged by their arch-opponents, Hayley Wickenheiser and her fellow Canadians. Of course those two teams have played a lot of close games—most of the U.S. players are descended from Canadian families. Even their equipment manager is named Brent Proulx.

It goes both ways, though. Cammi Granato, long-time scoring leader of the U.S. women's team, was the first woman to be elected to the Hockey Hall of Fame. Reversing the trend exemplified by Pierre Lamoureux, she crossed the border to play university hockey at Concordia University in Montreal while getting a degree in sports management, whatever that is. She graduated from Concordia 28 years after I left the place, if you can believe that! That year, 1997, it was announced that women's ice hockey would be an Olympic sport, so Cammi helped organize a U.S. national team, and played for them for years, becoming the best women's hockey player in the USA, or as they say down there, the world.

But Granato's Canadian experience was not over. Now she lives in North Vancouver with her husband Ray Ferraro, who came from Trail, an Interior of B.C. town that produces metal and sports stars. Ray Ferraro played for six NHL teams over 18 years, and got over 100 points twice. He and his wife would both get into hockey broadcasting.

Cammi is the sister of Tony Granato, who played 14 seasons in the NHL, and quite a few games against his future brother-in-law. Ray has a son playing pro hockey somewhere in the world, but he is not related to the Ferraro twins (to get back to our other topic). Chris and Peter Ferraro came from small-town Long Island, and had quite long careers as pro hockey players. Their chief claim to fame is that they were the second set of identical twins to suit up for the same NHL team, the New York Rangers. That happened in the 1995–96 season. During that season with the Rangers, one twin scored one goal and the other twin scored one assist.

Their professional playing days ended late in the 2008–09 season when they were toiling for the Las Vegas Wranglers of the East Coast Hockey League. In a typical East Coast game against the Alaska Aces, on March 24, the Ferraro twins joined in a brawl with a lot of other players, swinging sticks, falling down while trying to throw punches, cursing in a language known only to players who were no longer up in the American Hockey League. It took a long time to get the players and medics off the discoloured ice, and when they did, Chris went to the hospital with a broken leg, and a few days later Peter received a season's suspension for spearing an Ace.

Wisely, the Ferraro brothers decided to quit pro hockey and go into the hockey-school business back on Long Island.

The first set of identical twins to skate together in the NHL were two of the aforementioned Sutters. The Sutter clan from Viking, Alberta, sent six brothers to the NHL, where they lasted from 1976 till 2001 as players before most of them became coaches and managers. Even a few Sutters from the next generation made it to the majors for a couple of seasons. The Sutters were not fine artists the way Wayne Gretzky, say, was a fine artist. They tended to be those necessary teammates who would get in the way of people, hit them with something, or knock in a surprise goal to win an important game. None of them reached a thousand points, Brent Sutter being the most successful at 829.

The identical twins, Rich and Ron Sutter, were not identical in skill. Ron was drafted fourth in the 1982 entry draft, the highest any of the brothers had gone. Rich went tenth. Ron played for seven NHL teams in 19 seasons, and Rich played for seven teams in only 13 seasons. So it is not surprising that Ron scored over 200 goals, while Rich ended up with 149.

But all these journeymen Sutters, energetic and determined, a long way from dreamboats on the handsomeness scale, were always indulged by the fans, and tolerated by the fans in other rinks. Who could hate a Sutter?

The only other North American twins to make it to the NHL are Kris and Ryan Russell. If you can't quite place them, you are not in a minority. From their first names, of course, you can deduce that they are pretty recent. They were born in 1987, while the Sutters were grunting around big league rinks. The village they grew up in, Caroline, Alberta, has about 200 houses in it, which make it half as big as Viking.

It quite often happens that one twin has a lot more of a certain talent than does the other. A lot of people know that the Cuban-American home-run hitter and steroids-and-guns fan Jose Canseco got 462 Major League home runs before they made him quit. But how many know that his twin brother, Ozzie, who was not in later years as big as Jose, holds the independent Atlantic League record for home runs in a season? However, in his severely abbreviated Major League career he got 462 fewer homers than did his brother.

The Russell twins are sort of like that. Not that either of them is as illustrious as Jose Canseco. Ryan has spent most of his career in the minors and Europe, suiting up for 41 games with the Columbus Blue Jackets in 2011–12, managing two points as a defensive centre. Kris was on that team with him for a few games before he got traded, and then he got traded again, and the last time I looked he was an alternate captain for the Calgary Flames. As a defenceman, Kris scored 30 goals during his first seven years in the league.

As I said, there's no great sin in not knowing the story of the Russell twins. Or the Columbus Blue Jackets, for that matter.

There have been three other sets of identical twins in the NHL, and they are all from Sweden. What is it about Sweden? The Swedish national women's soccer team features the Karlsson twins, Elin and Nellie. There's some punk music group called the Swedish Twins, but I don't know whether they are Swedish. Maybe they're from Columbus. "Swedish twins" is a slang term indicating two albino people who are close and dependent on one another to make it in this world. A few years ago some Swedish twins tried to commit suicide on social media. There were also some twin Indonesian girls who were adopted by separate Swedish couples and raised a few kilometres from each other until they met one another in their thirties. Years and years ago there were some Swedish twin women who went crazy and killed people in England after hearing strange messages from each other in their heads.

Well, everyone knows that twins are strange. And if you have read Swedish novels and poetry and seen Bergman's films, you know that Swedes can be strange too.

But they can sure play hockey.

Look at the Lundqvist twins, Joel and Henrik. They were born the year that Rich and Ron Sutter were taken in the entry draft. Like some of the people we have been discussing, Joel was a non-scoring forward, and that sort of thing does not excite Texans, so he lasted for a few years in Dallas, before going to his present club, Frölunda, where every year he registers more penalties than points. His twin brother, Henrik, though, has been the New York Rangers MVP for the past seven years, at this writing. When they were kids, his brother tricked him into being a goalie, perhaps never imagining that he would become the best goalie in Sweden on his way to becoming the best goalie in the NHL and an Olympic champion.

Or consider the Sundström twins, Peter and Patrik, of a generation earlier. Unlike the Lundqvists, they were born into a hockey family, but like the Lundqvists they had unequal records of success in the NHL. Peter played forward for three teams on the Atlantic coast and wound up with 145 points in 338 games before returning to his home country to play for Malmö. It's a nice city, Malmö. But I joined quite a few people in paying more attention to Patrik Sundström. I did so because he played for the Vancouver Canucks in the early eighties, and everyone else did so because he was the best Sundström on the ice.

Just about any success that the Vancouver Canucks have had has been due to their wisdom in signing Swedish hockey players. It's a good thing that they didn't have Don Cherry for owner or general manager. Almost all my interest in the Canucks has been caused by the guys from Sweden, and there have been a lot of them. Patrik Sundström took his place in a tradition started by Thomas Gradin and Lars Lindgren in 1978 and continued by Markus Näslund, Mattias Öhlund, Alex Edler and a couple of guys named Sedin. They even had the great Mats Sundin for a few months at the end of his fabulous career.

Let me put it this way about Patrik Sundström: he set some Vancouver Canucks records, and he even set some Vancouver Canucks playoff records. In those days you didn't often get a chance to set Vancouver Canucks playoff records.

And then along came the Sedins. I think that a lot of people will nominate the Sedins as the best twin act ever in any sport.

When the Sedins started playing for the Vancouver Canucks in 2000, anyone with an unjaundiced eye could see that these young men from Örnsköldsvik were adults skating among adolescents.

The manner in which the Canucks managed to get both Sedins was extremely complicated and involved deals made with Chicago, Atlanta and Tampa Bay. The Canucks had been awful as usual in 1999, and were prepared to take Henrik with their first draft pick, then make all kinds of pick trades that called for promises that the other bad teams would not snatch Daniel out of their hands. Of course the twins wanted to play on the same line, something they had done for three years of pro hockey in Sweden, and years of amateur hockey before that.

Twins on the forward line? It was intriguing, and for some people, exciting. Coming at a time when I was beginning to quit following football and hockey, the signing got me interested in watching Vancouver games, at least on TV. In fact, now in their fourteenth season (they spent a season in Sweden while the NHL players were on strike for more millions of dollars), I read the Canucks box score to see how many points they got the night before. Fourteenth season! The Sedins have set a lot of records, but maybe this one is somehow the most indicative: since they started NHL play more than 14 years ago, neither of them has played one game for another NHL team. I like that. I'm reminded of Jean Béliveau, of Henri Richard, of George Armstrong. Put it another way: of Joe DiMaggio, of Ted Williams, of Stan Musial.

In those four years before the players' strike, the Sedins played really entertaining two-way hockey, but they did not exhibit stratospheric scoring statistics. To the normal barstool hockey fans in Vancouver, they were not satisfactory. In fact, most Vancouver hockey fans wanted them to be traded, hopefully for some big bruising goal-scoring guys who maybe didn't speak English as well as these Swedes, but who knew what the Canadian hockey fan wanted—more hitting, more goals and fewer abstract words. The sports press and broadcasters were not Sedin fans, either. How did Canucks management fall for this deal, they wanted to know.

Some guy in a clown suit on the *Hockey Night in Canada* between-periods broadcast allowed as to how he had told you so—these Europeans, and especially these neutral Swedes, eat quiche instead of steak before games. He preferred good tough Canadian lads such as Todd Bertuzzi. And the Vancouver press did not refute the Couch's coroner. More and more the term "Sedin Sisters" was heard around Vancouver.

What a bunch of idiots, I said at the time.

Remember Archie Moore in Edmonton, getting tired of the know-nothing booers in the arena, and TKOing Sonny Andrews? Are you one of those folks who used to say, well, Ichiro Suzuki is a great singles hitter, but he's a singles hitter, huh? The day after some such remark in the *Seattle Times* or on some open yap radio show, Suzuki would hit five consecutive home runs during batting practice.

After the Sedins came back from their year in Sweden, they started taking over the offence for the Canucks. They did not achieve Gretzkyan numbers, but they resembled Gretzky as playmakers. There has never been a pair of twins or even siblings who seemed so much to employ extra sensory perception in knowing where the other brother's stick blade was going to be. The Telepathy Brothers, I called them on the occasions I got to watch them skate. It got to be so that one didn't want to see them sit down between shifts. What's the fun of watching a Vancouver Canucks shift with no Sedins on it?

In 1999–2000, they had played their last pre-NHL season for their Swedish team, Modo Hockey, finishing first and second in team scoring. Now, in their second post-Modo season they decided to show the skeptics in Vancouver and around the league how good they could get. Their point totals took an upward leap, and in the 2009–10 season, Henrik the centre got 83 assists in 82 games, and won the Art Ross Trophy as the league's highest points-getter at 112. He was also awarded the Hart Trophy as the league's most valuable player. He led the Canucks to win the Presidents' Trophy as the best team in the West. In the playoffs he got 14 points in 12 games. *The Sporting News* made him their player of the year. In that contest and in the Hart Trophy contest, he bested Alex Ovechkin and Sidney Crosby.

At the beginning of the 2010–11 season, the Canucks made Henrik their new captain.

I don't think he starred in that year's *Rock 'em Sock 'em* video.

A lot of people may have forgotten that Daniel Sedin missed 19 games in that season of 2009–10. He got 85 points in 63 games. Next year he would again have 22 more points than games played, with even better results.

During that season a person could not help wondering whether Henrik was doing everything he could to help his brother succeed him as Art Ross guy. Since their child-hood Daniel had been the sniper and Henrik the set-up man. In 2010–11 Daniel got his highest ever assist total and Henrik's point total dropped by 18. Daniel finished first in the league with 101 points, and Henrik got 94 for fourth place. In addition to the Art Ross Trophy, Daniel was a finalist for the Hart Trophy, finishing second to an Anaheim forward named Corey Perry, who scored 50 goals. The sportswriters like the idea of 50 goals in a season. The league's players, who vote for the Ted Lindsay Trophy, chose Daniel Sedin as their player of the year.

For the next two years the Sedins scored just under a point a game, but in 2013–14 their totals took a dip. After the team was swept out of the 2013 playoffs, management fired Alain Vigneault, possibly the best coach they had ever had, and replaced him with an unusual human being named John Tortorella, who had been fired by the New York Rangers. The Rangers jumped at the chance to hire Vigneault, whose Canucks had finished first in the Northwest Division six of the last seven years. That year Vigneault got his Rangers into the Stanley Cup Final, while Tortorella, who had had three divisional first places in his career, led the Canucks from first place down to last.

Tortorella was not the only problem in that season. The owners and management went all fumblefingers when it came to making trades and protecting the salary cap. Roberto Luongo, a veteran whose lifetime record puts him about in the middle of the pack when it comes to NHL goaltenders, but whom the Vancouver sports reporters and fans always thought was a premium goalie, was occasionally seen with a smile on his face, but it was a ruefully ironic smile.

Tortorella was high on the list of problems, though. He came on as a tough taskmaster in training camp, and made his players pass difficult physical tests and conditioning standards. He stated his aim to make this a new kind of Canucks team—no more streamlined rushing and prodigious shooting; this would be a team that scraped people against the boards. Players were going to fall in front of more slapshots. The Sedins were going to be used for penalty-killing. Sure, said the Sedins, we want to be complete hockey players. At the end of the 2013–14 season, Henrik had 50 points. Daniel had 46.

In 2014–15, Roberto Luongo had gone back to Miami. Willie Desjardins was the coach. The Canucks had the highest point total in the league and the Sedins were each scoring a point a game. Now the Vancouver hockey scribes and the fans let us know that they had always loved these twins, and congratulated each other for bringing them to the Canucks in the first place.

WE'RE NOT *in* MONTREAL ANYMORE, TOTO

Okay, we were living in a nice little house in Kitsilano in the summer of 1971. The commune's other five people (plus baby) had moved west a block or two on York Avenue, to a big old house they planned on buying. We were here on York, Angela pregnant to beat the band and poet George Stanley occupying the upstairs. There were traditions abuilding. One was pub night, a once-a-week affair at the taproom of the Cecil Hotel, where writers from out of town knew that they could meet their local counterparts. Another was the brand-new Kosmic League, a guerrilla anti-organized softball league funded by the Liberal Party's grants that were designed to keep young people from being rioters and nogoodniks—Opportunities for Youth (OFY) and Local Initiatives Projects (LIP). Our team was the Granville Grange Zephyrs, a bunch of painters and writers, a few of them former teammates on the York Street Tigers in Montreal.

As for the household: I was meeting people from time to time to see whether I was going to get a job teaching at the five-year-old Simon Fraser University, and Angela was growing more and more pregnant. George Stanley, having recently moved to Vancouver from San Francisco, as other poets had, got jobs at the *Georgia Straight*, at that time an underground newspaper, and Duthie Books, the main bookstore downtown. I don't remember whether I went to any ice hockey games in the 1971–72 season.

I do remember that the feeling in Vancouver was a lot different from the feeling in Montreal. For one thing, people in Montreal just plain expected their team to do very well. So it had been since the National Hockey League began. The Canadiens would have won their first Stanley Cup in 1919, but the finals between Montreal and Seattle were called off due to the worldwide flu epidemic. They had to wait till 1924 to get their first cup, but by the middle of the century they were winning them in clusters. The Canadiens were becoming the New York Yankees of the NHL, except for one thing: they weren't winning for Satan. Between 1956 and 1971, the year I left town, they won 10 out of 16 Stanley Cups. Between 1976 and 1979 they would win four more. The Vancouver Canucks, by contrast, entered the league in 1970, and in their 40-odd seasons have played in the Stanley Cup Finals thrice, losing every time.

Every year, after the first month of play, Canucks fans get all excited. When I was a university professor, I used to tell the fans who happened to be enrolled in my classes that the 'Nucks would go without a win in February. Something like that happened almost every year.

Of course, when I took up residence on the west coast in 1971, they were just finishing their first season. The powers that start up hockey enthusiasm were doing their work. There were some old-timey fans who used to follow the Canucks when they were in the Western Hockey League, but now we were big league, if you can innocently call hockey big league, and parents were promoting excitement in their kids. What they call minor hockey sprang up all over the lower mainland. Rinks started operating in the dark of early morning from Ladner to Chilliwack. Canucks jerseys started showing up on torsos everywhere, exhibiting an amateurish logo that somehow featured a rink and a hockey stick and still tried to suggest the letter C. If you looked around those rinks, you saw that most of the little ankle-skaters were shooting right. If you are going to find yourself with one hand on the end of the stick, as when poke-checking, you want it in your dominant hand, after all. Get that, Mum?

So I was feeling as if I had flung myself a few thousand miles away from real hockey. The Vancouver Canucks were bringing real NHL teams to town for visits, but the locals seemed somehow like the black-and-white Canadian comic books of the wartime years—kind of amateurish, sort of like books published in small towns in the Cariboo.

Of course having a new baby, and a first baby at that, I was not about to find the time or money to go to hockey games in the Pacific Coliseum way out there near the Pacific National Exhibition and the racetrack. But every once in a while the NHL would sneak its way into the mind games I always played while waiting to go to sleep: I would think of the alphabet and the hockey names strung along it. Sometimes this childlike exercise would find its way into my diary, as on Friday, February 4, 1972: Steve Atkinson, Bob Baun, Yvan Cournoyer, Dave Dryden, Phil Esposito, Norm Ferguson, Ted Green, Bryan Hextall, Ted Irvine, Bob Johnson, Cliff Koroll, Guy Lafleur, Stan Mikita, Lou Nanne, Murray Oliver, Rosaire Paiement, Bobby Rousseau, Glen Sather, Ted Taylor, Garry Unger, Ed Van Impe, Dunc Wilson.

You will notice that I let myself off the hook when it came to a few of the letters. I probably didn't even know about the Sabres' Rod Zaine or remember the Canucks' Pat Quinn. I tended to be more demanding of myself with my other alphabetical lists—baseball players, rivers of the world, movie stars, novel titles and so on. When I was doing former NHL players, I was always grateful for the Quackenbushes.

You will have noticed that I was running something like a solo campaign in the old study-hall game that Joe Makse and I used to play, naming every player in the league instead of the stuff we were supposed to know for grade 10 social studies.

It's too bad that there were not a lot of ice surfaces in Vancouver in 1972. We writers and artists might have added hockey to the baseball and basketball leagues we had invented. But I kind of doubt it.

As soon as you say both "hockey" and "1972" you think about the so-called "Summit Series" that was famously ended by a goal that the flaks will never let you forget, the one they call the "most famous goal in Canadian hockey history." Paul Henderson, a pretty fair Maple Leafs forward, managed that marker in Moscow to prove to Canadians that we are still the best hockey country in the world, a feat that would be commemorated on collector plates and Canadian postage stamps for at least a half-century to come.

If you are as old as I am, you'll remember that Canada won Olympic ice hockey games 24–0, and then you'll remember the Soviets deciding on hockey as politics by other means, until the glorious Penticton Vees beat them back in 1955. For the next 15 years or so, the Reds kept getting better, and despite their poorly made uniforms, they gained respect all over the Western world as a highly superior hockey machine. You will remember, if you are nearly as old as I am, that they would knock us off in some big tournament, and all our hockey people would say that the Soviets were really professionals, and what chance did we have while we insisted on sending amateur teams to the Olympics and the International Ice Hockey Federation World Championships?

It was a bit like communism and capitalism. The Soviet hockey teams were all state-sponsored, so of course anyone they sent to the tournament would be a branch of the government. On the other hand, all the independently owned and operated Canadian teams had to compete for the chance to go up against the commies. The Soviets' first success came right after they decided to take to the international ice, their first World Championship coming in 1954, just when the Cold War had got going in earnest.

By the way, the term "Cold War" is generally credited to George Orwell, who invented the term to describe the condition in which people would have to live under the threat of atomic weapons owned by one nation. See his essay "You and the Atomic Bomb," first published in 1945. The term was first used by French writers in the thirties, but by 1947, it had come to mean the rivalry and proxy military adventures of Washington and Moscow, or NATO and the Warsaw Pact. Of course, when China started making boom-boom, the term shifted around, and its first large battlefield was Korea between 1950 and 1953.

A year after the ceasefire in Korea, then, the Soviets went to neutral Sweden and beat the Canadians and announced that they were now a dominant player in the game. Between 1954 and 1971 the Soviets would emerge as winners 11 times. The Canadians? Four times.

"Damn it, if those Russkies ever had to face our NHL players they would soon find out just how much further they have to go," averred the Canadian Olympic Committee.

"Truer words were never said," said more than one NHL team owner.

"Sure as shit," said a lot of the Canadian players.

"Yer darn tootin'," said Howie Meeker.

The 1970 World Championships were supposed to happen in Canada, but the new national organization called Hockey Canada said enough is enough, and pulled out of the tournament. How embarrassing! Or what brinkmanship! Thanks goodness this was ice hockey and not planes and tanks. Okay, said the International Ice Hockey

Federation, we will hold the 1970 games in Sweden. The Soviets won in 1970, and again in 1971, and in the 1972 Olympics. The Canadians? Who remembered them?

Hockey people and the corporations that liked to make a profit by selling things to hockey fans figured that the IIHF was too slow in following the golf and tennis functionaries down the path to open competition. (Open competition is another word for professional competition.) They kept saying that the NHL would kick the Big Red Machine out of the rink, and they hoped that they would get quoted in the Soviet press. Sure enough, Moscow, who had beaten the West into space, now hinted that they would like a bigger challenge for their skaters.

The notion of a big Soviet-Canadian series was leaked to *Izvestia*, and not just to the sports pages. The Canadian papers leaked the leak. The heat was turned on in the back rooms. While the Canadianless World Championship tournament was taking place in Prague in April 1972, the guys from Ottawa and the guys from Moscow got to talking about a big series between the best Soviet players and the best (professional) Canadian players.

Hockey fans in Montreal and Winnipeg squirmed when they heard the rumours.

"Let us at 'em," they whispered.

The arrangements were made in true Cold War style, the sneaky Russians trying to make sure that their national team got as many advantages as possible, the naive and eager Canadians so sure of their superiority that they made concession after concession. The first four games would be played in Montreal, Toronto, Winnipeg and Vancouver, and the last four games would be played in

Moscow, on the wider ice. The games would be played under international rules and mediated by European refs, under the two-referee European system. The series would be played in September, before the North American training camps.

"Hell," said a fan in Toronto, "let them put seven men on the ice. We'll still steal their ugly shorts."

You could feel the anticipation all across the Dominion. At last those uppity Ivans were going to get shocked into reality.

Because of the way the sports pages and the *Hockey News* operate, Canadians did not know who the Soviet players were. But they sure knew who the Canadians were. There was no way a bunch of guys with "off" at the ends of their names were going to skate with people named:

> *Phil Esposito*
> *Gilbert Perreault*
> *Jean Ratelle*
> *Bobby Clarke*
> *Stan Mikita*
> *Frank Mahovlich*
> *Guy Lapointe*
> *Vic Hadfield*
> *Rod Gilbert*
> *Brad Park*
> *Yvan Cournoyer*
> *Paul Henderson*
> *Ron Ellis*
> *Serge Savard*
> *Wayne Cashman*
> *Peter Mahovlich*

Rod Seiling

Mickey Redmond

Bill White

Dennis Hull

Gary Bergman

Bill Goldsworthy

Pat Stapleton

Don Awrey

J. P. Parisé

Red Berenson

Bobby Orr travelled with the team but did not play. Some other greats made it into the warm-up games against the Swedes and the Czechs, these including Marcel Dionne, Dale Tallon and Rick Martin.

In goal the Reds had to face Tony Esposito and Ken Dryden, and just in case, Eddie Johnston was there with his equipment. Things looked scary for the no-name squad. I mean who'd ever heard of Vyacheslav Solodukhin?

Maybe Vladislav Tretiak was good enough in the net to stop those robotic Soviet forwards with their fancy crisscross skating game, but the Montreal Forum crowd wouldn't be able to offer him anything but their pity. He was just lucky that the Rocket and Boom Boom and Béliveau weren't going to be swooping down on him.

It wasn't as if Canadians didn't know anything about these Soviet people; they had been able to read the scores, at least, from the tourneys they kept on winning mainly because the Canadians were boycotting them. But the sportswriters and fans and players all knew that it took tough kids in a free-enterprise world to make it past all the competition to the top of the hockey world, which meant playing for businesses such as the Chicago Black Hawks or the Toronto Maple Leafs. Famous Western hockey analysts predicted that the Russkies would lose all eight games. Alan Eagleson said that Canadians should hang their heads if we didn't win every game.

Somehow, that famously shifty lawyer and future jailbird wormed his way into power and became the public face for the Canadian side. At first he didn't get it: he wanted his team to be called the NHL All-Stars, and had to be informed that it was to be an all-Canadian team. In an era during which the Liberal Party of Canada had learned that it was a good idea to use names for things that would make sense in French, Trans-Canada Air Lines had changed its name to Air Canada (1965), and Royal Mail Canada had changed its contentious brand. So Team Canada it was.

Eagleson's position was complicated at the least, dicey, some people would say. Every time you turned around, there he was, a lawyer for Bobby Orr and other moneymakers, head of the players' union, confidante of the NHL owners and fellow diner with various highfalutin' businessmen in Canadian and U.S. cities. Hockey folks so much wanted the deal to go through that they ignored any possible conflict of interest. Hell, it was a dogfight of interests. If you want to know more about the ways in which Mr. Eagleson could earn himself a lot of invisible money, have a read of *Orr: My Story* (2013).

But the future member of the Hockey Hall of Fame and the Order of Canada (both of which he no longer is a member of) promoted the hell out of the tournament, going back on deals that had been made before he arrived, and threatening the foreigners with cancellation (and maybe worse). In mid-August, Team Canada's 35 skaters and hobblers went into training camp for the next three weeks, with Eagleson's choice, Harry Sinden, as their coach.

"Where the hell is Bobby Hull?" a lot of people asked. "Where is Gerry Cheevers?"

"Gone to the WHA," they were told, "along with some other damned good hockey players."

"So what?" they asked. "This is Team Canada, not Team NHL."

"This is business," they were told.

These were business people who wanted to promote the idea that the World Hockey Association was an "outlaw league."

Besides it wasn't as if the Soviets were going to be able to skate with Team Canada.

On September 2, they skated circles around them.

It started the way most Canadians thought it would. Phil Esposito won the first faceoff, and 30 seconds later he bullied his way to Frank Mahovlich's rebound to score the tournament's first goal. A few minutes later the pretty fair Maple Leaf Paul Henderson bumped a slow puck past the Russian goalie. Poor guy, that 20-year-old named Tretiak. The 18,000 fans in the Forum settled in for a dozen Canadian goals and looked forward to a shutout for their own goalie Ken Dryden, who a few months before had won the Calder Trophy as rookie of the year in the NHL.

But as the first period progressed, the Canadian skaters were coming off the ice a little gassed. Maybe the three weeks of training camp were not energetic enough, or maybe not long enough, given that the Soviet players were used to keeping in top shape all year. By the end of the first period the score was 2–2. I and the other couple million people watching on *Hockey Night in the Free World* began to get a little edgy. After two periods, the visitors were up 4–2. In the third, Bobby Clarke, the kid from Manitoba with a gummy smile, got a goal off a scramble, but then the Soviets, now aware that the NHL players were not the supermen they had believed them to be, skated by their panting opponents and breezed to a 7–3 rout. It was so quiet in the Forum that you could hear the Canadian defencemen gasping for air as someone with a "v" at the end of his name took the puck away and passed it across the ice. Recollecting that night, Paul Henderson said that he and his teammates had never seen a transition game such as the one they were just introduced to.

In the pre-Gretzky and the post-Gretzky eras, the Canadian offensive game mainly consisted of dumping the puck in and racing for control of it with a lot of hope in your heart and good enough aim to bodycheck the enemy into the boards. On that warm September night the guys in the scratchy-looking uniforms were always skating and skating and passing the puck back and forth so fast that the other guys could not bash them, and eventually there would be an open place on the ice, and there would be a Soviet hockey player with a stick ready to snap it by a sophomore goalie. They were playing hockey like basketball.

Someday someone ought to write a short story about some guys sitting in a beer parlour in Parry Sound, discussing what they had just spent two and a half hours watching on the bar's new colour TV. Like everyone else who watched the game on TV, they had become less sure of Canadian dominance on the ice, and were beginning to get interested in this team of indefatigable Slavs. Eleven years earlier we in the West had had our heads turned around by Yuri Gagarin and Gherman Titov, the first men in space. In the years to come we were going to hear a lot more about Valeri Kharlamov, Vladimir Petrov, Boris Mikhailov, Alexander Maltsev and my personal favourite, Alexander Yakushev.

Game 2 in Toronto was a different story. Harry Sinden gave up his plan to dazzle the visitors with speed and artistry, and brought on the tough guys, benching skilled players such as Rod Gilbert and Jean Ratelle, replacing them with the more pugilistic Bill White and Wayne Cashman. Fight fans were happy. Hockey fans, your humble servant included, were disappointed. The Russians still tried to skate and pass. The Canadians replied with mauling and smashing. The referees were two USAmericans who were happy to let infractions short of attempted murder go. The home team won the game 4–1. I began to cheer for the visitors.

So the series was evened, and thoughts of a Canadian series win crept back into some reporters' heads. Fans who preferred street rumbles to Russian ballet cheered Wayne Cashman as the Canadians went ahead in game three in Winnipeg. But the Soviets wisely chose not to play the Canadian style of individual power, opting to play as a team, the puck never staying on any stick blade for longer than a blink. The tough guys went ahead by two goals, but the game ended in a 4–4 tie. More and more hockey followers were growing to dislike the way the Canadian coach and individual players had decided the game had to be played. They were even starting to cheer for the flying

Slavs. In the fourth game, played in Vancouver, these sentiments were expressed by Canadians sitting in the Pacific Coliseum. I was one of them.

I have never seen a Stanley Cup game in person, but when the Chicago Bulls played the Seattle Supersonics for the 1996 NBA championship, I saw games 3, 4 and 5 in Seattle. Better than that: I had free tickets because Luc Longley was the Bulls' starting center, and I was a friend of his father and stepmother. The only drawback was that I had to sit with the Bulls' relatives and girlfriends. I was not as loud as I usually am at a sporting event.

I saw game 4 of the Summit Series free, too. I am not sure of the details behind this fortunate fact. Maybe Hockey Canada had to paper the house because Vancouver fans were not as rabid as Montreal fans. My hockey-playing poet friend Lionel Kearns showed up with a free ticket for me, and when we arrived at the Pacific Coliseum we found that we would be sitting with a bunch of rimesters. Apparently someone who was working with the hockey people was given a batch of tickets and told to find people who would fill those seats behind the south goal. Even Robin Blaser, the elegant poet formerly of San Francisco, was there. Blaser was the sort of poet you would expect to be more likely to attend a production of *Les Sylphildes* than to catch a game between large hockey players from Canada and the USSR.

But Blaser was enchanted. We were lucky that the goal we were sitting above and behind was the one tended for the first and third periods by Vladimir Tretiak, the 20-year-old newlywed, who spent the night as he had spent the series, reaching out with hand or foot or stick to nip a disk of rubber that made its almost invisible way to within a centimetre of the goal line. This was the first hockey game Robin Blaser had ever seen, and how could we explain to him that it was a far cry from the usual pedestrian thump party we saw too often on *HNIC*? The Canadian team tried to convert it into one of those, but the flying Soviet forwards hadn't won a game since Montreal, and they were getting used to the narrow Canadian rink.

I envied Blaser his first experience of the colours and the sounds, though I wished that it were midwinter in Montreal rather than early fall in Vancouver. The bright red-and-white uniforms, the hiss of blades on the whitened surface, the almost-fearful bang of a slapshot against the end boards, even the smell of artificial ice that fills the memory banks of most Canadians, made me wonder why I didn't go to hockey games anymore.

But the way the Canadians played reminded me. The two Americans who had refereed the Winnipeg game were no longer with us, so at least the home team could not carry handguns; but they had sticks and elbows. During the Montreal game it had become obvious that Team Canada could not skate with the Soviets. Since then Harry Sinden had encouraged them to try to cow the foreigners and get them off their feet one way or another while people like Mahovlich and Esposito tried to slam the puck past the youngster in the Soviet cage. There were a few exceptions, notably Paul Henderson, who played the best hockey of his life and found a knack for popping in the winning goal, as he did in the sixth, seventh and most famously, the eighth game. He was the opposite of Bobby Clarke, whose main purpose was apparently to break his opponents' legs with roundhouse slashes.

But at least Bobby Clarke was no sissy. Like almost all the Canadian players he played with a bare head. Those chickenshit Russians were all wearing helmets. You didn't see Esposito and Clarke and White wearing helmets. Well, Paul Henderson did. But what were those commies trying to do? Make it look as if the Canadians were aiming to hurt them on purpose? The referees did all they could to keep the penalty differential as slim as possible. If they had stuck to the rules, there would have been a bigger gap between their totals—Canada 147 minutes; USSR 84 minutes.

As the series unfolded on television that September, there was an interesting development in the audience's response. The patriotism that our press and business people had built up began to be replaced by a love of hockey. The previously unknown Soviet players began to gather Canadian fans; this was especially true of Tretiak, who was not only valiant between the pipes for all eight games, but also had a name people could pronounce. Sitting in the arena in Vancouver, one could hear spectators cheer for Tretiak, especially the poets behind him, and offer negative reactions to the goons, especially Bill Goldsworthy, who got his teammates down 2–0 early in the first period. Goldsworthy, inserted into the lineup to "add energy," was called for cross-checking in the second minute of the game. The great Boris Mikhailov scored a power-play goal. On his next shift Goldsworthy gave elbowing a try. Boris Mikhailov scored another power play goal. Oh no, figured the Canadian side, before this game gets totally out of hand, we'd better get more "physical." Apparently the "mental" hadn't worked out.

See, if Team Canada were to win in Vancouver, they would head to Moscow up a game. Lose, and they would fly over the pole and land a game down. So what did they do, as the boos from the crowd grew louder and longer? Two things. They increased the thuggery, and shot as often as they could, usually from just inside the blue line. In the third period alone they shot 23 times, often from nearby cities. Boo, said the crowd. I even booed Frank Mahovlich when I saw him sitting on a Soviet defenceman who was laboring to get out from under him; Bobby Clarke waved his stick in the face of any Soviet player who had more teeth than he did. The Soviets played so well as a group (or machine, the capitalists in the crowd would say) that they made their hosts look like a pickup team of puck-hogs.

Head office officials for Team Canada were feeling thankful that there were no more home games. If there had been they might have tried to move the venue to Whitehorse.

In the stands uneasiness gave way to disappointment and then disappointment gave way to something like anger. In the middle of the first period a few boos were heard for Goldsworthy's second "mistake." In the second period there was applause for both teams, but as time went by the boos became more noticeable. The boos followed every mugging committed by Sinden's gang. When the Canadians left the ice, after a few unpleasant gestures meant for the winners, it almost seemed as if the entire crowd of 15,000 were sounding its displeasure. When Tretiak was announced as one of the game's three stars, a great cheer celebrated our new hero.

Phil Esposito didn't get it. He thought that the fans were booing because the Canadians were losing the series. I was there—I know that the fans were booing because they did not want to be represented by a bunch of thugs. On nationwide television we would hear the incensed Esposito complaining. "We gave our best," he said. If that was your best, Vancouver thought, we would hate to see your worst. "We can't believe the bad press we've got, the booing we've got in our own building. We came out because we love our country."

He just did not get it. He must have thought that it is perfectly good Canadian behaviour to play like hoodlums. He must have been far removed from any sense of good sportsmanship and decency. "My country, right or wrong," he must have thought.

Meanwhile, on the streets of Moscow a new slang term arose. A person who acted like an unsocialized brute was called an "Esposito."

But you know what happened a few weeks later when the Canadian team played the last four games in the Luzhniki Ice Palace in Moscow. All four games were won by one goal. The Soviets went behind 3–0 in the first, and won 5–4. Gilbert Perreault gave up and went home. The Canadians were going to have to win the remaining three games, in Russia, surrounded by reporters and crowds who thought they were monsters. There were quite a few Canadians who had flown to Moscow to support the guys who were doing their best.

Paul Henderson scored a goal in that game 5, and then got all those winning goals. He almost made up for Bobby Clarke, who made sure that the Soviets' most dangerous offensive threat would not be able to play in the last game. Henderson was quoted in the press as stating that Clarke's slashing of Valeri Kharlamov was the low point of the series. Unfortunately, he took it back a while later, even though Clarke was to admit that he was trying to break the flashy Soviet player's leg, and that he was doing it at the request of assistant coach John Ferguson. Much has been made of Henderson's last goal, including coins and medals and stamps and paintings. He was, indeed, the hero of the Summit Series, not because of the famous goal, but because of his fair and decent play.

Sitting in front of our television set at an ungodly hour, I cheered for Paul Henderson, and then turned off the TV set, announcing that I was never again going to watch Canadian ice hockey.

HOCKEY
DUDS

I have been thinking of the second-rate equipment and scratchy old woolen sweaters the Soviet team wore in the 1972 season. I seem to have sensitive skin and a real aversion to scratchy clothes. I just cringe when I see those lucky people who can wear sweaters on their bare skin. I am reminded of the time when my Kootenays grandmother died, and my grandfather gave me four things: a little rat terrier with a big *S*-shaped scar on her back (this was Dinky, who used her skinny little legs to walk with me for prodigious distances in the hills, and who stopped from time to time to have a litter of pups—nobody kept a leash on their dogs in Oliver when I was a kid), a pair of little bronze cowboy boots that had an ad for the Calgary Stampede on it for a while, *Stairs of Sand*, a novel by Zane Grey, and a pair of herringbone tweed trousers.

My parents made me wear these trousers whenever I went to Sunday school or with my other grandmother to church in Summerland. They were torturously itchy on my bare legs, and I suffered greatly while exercising my faith, especially in the hot summertime long before air conditioning came to the Valley. I knew that I could have worn long underwear, but it would have made the heat even worse, besides which I hadn't had a pair of long underwear since leaving Greenwood, B.C., when I was seven, plus the fact that long underwear would have added embarrassment to my itchiness. As soon as I got home, after eons of delay that were not my fault, I got those herringbones off my poor thin white legs.

But remember when I had a Toronto Maple Leafs adjustable ring, and a document showing that I was officially afflicted with the Toronto Maple Leafs Hockey Club? Well, courtesy of the Eaton's catalogue I had a blue sweater with the official insignia of my favourite hockey team. I wore it all winter, making sure that I had a shirt that covered every part of my body that a heavy sweater could reach. If I did anything strenuous, of course, I would sweat, and that is not something one enjoys doing inside a bulky sweater. Even worse were the times when the sweater would get soaked and heavy because of melting snow, or when a person fell through thin ice on the lake and we had to get him free. But I liked that blue-and-white sweater, and when my slightly younger buddy Billy Lyttle got one a year later, I was secretly glad that mine looked better because his maple leaf had been made hurriedly and cheaply, a piece of white felt with a simple leaf design dyed on it.

I don't remember whether I put on that sweater to express my loyalty, and sway the hockey gods while listening to Foster Hewitt's peculiar Ontario accent on *Hockey Night in Canada and Newfoundland*. I probably didn't. I probably didn't even run and get my adjustable Maple Leafs ring. Maybe I would have dressed for the occasion if I had had one of the tops they have nowadays, those light smooth jerseys made of some miracle fabric.

Billy and I were probably not the only Maple Leafs in town, but I don't remember seeing any Red Wings or Rangers, not for another decade, anyway. Nowadays you see people in jerseys and caps and scarves bearing all the NHL logos. Back in the day, when pennants were all the rage, kids like me had Maple Leafs pennants on our bedroom walls, along with those glow-in-the-dark pictures of Jesus.

There are so many logos nowadays, not just for sports teams but for political parties, beers, All-Star Games and fighter squadrons. For each sport I like to have my opinion of the best and worst uniforms and logos. As a veteran sports fan I lean toward classical simplicity. I hate to admit it, but in the National Football League, the best uniform belongs to the Dallas Cowboys. In baseball, and again I hate to admit it, the best uniform belongs to the New York Yankees. In the NBA it's got to be the Boston Celtics. You see what I mean about classic simplicity? In the Canadian Football League the bestselling souvenir clothing denotes the team in the smallest market, the Saskatchewan Roughriders.

You know that I have been leading up to the best uniform in the NHL. You already know—it's worn by the Detroit Red Wings.

Several outfits, such as the Philadelphia Flyers and the

Hells Angels have tried to do something with feathers, but Hockey Town was the first and is still the best.

There are a lot of terrible-looking jerseys in the minor leagues and the juniors, but there have been some bad ones even where the big money is. You might suggest the recent Los Angeles Kings designs, for example, or on the other coast, a swirl that is supposed to indicate bad weather. But really, I have to turn my head away when I see a picture of some Florida Panther. For one thing, the uniform has to carry just about every colour in the spectrum, including brown. I think that panther is brown, or maybe khaki. That big cat is the main problem; he or she is made to suffer extreme perspective, so we see a huge head and huge front paws with gigantic claws above dinky back legs. I guess it is meant to be leaping toward you, but it kind of looks as if it had been squeezed out of a panther tube.

I have seen worse. Have you ever watched a game in the Swedish league? I was teaching in Denmark in 1995, and I didn't watch very much TV, but when I could, I liked to watch the Norwegian women's handball team playing international matches. Once, though, I caught an ice hockey game from Sweden. If you think that the growing menace of advertising in our rinks is awful, you would hate the ones in Malmö and Göteborg. There is, as there is in Philadelphia and San Jose, advertising on the boards and the ice. In Sweden you will also see advertising on the pipes on either side of the goalkeeper. There is advertising on the ice machine. The players themselves look a little like racecar drivers. You can pick out the name of the team and maybe of the player, but in trying to do so you will see the names of a lot of commercial outfits.

That's the way in Europe, in all their sports. One of their kowtowings has made its way around the world—you have to look really closely at any professional soccer jersey to see what football club it represents. I usually give up and just cheer for Fly Emirates or Hyundai.

I don't remember wearing a lot of NHL clothes after my Leafs sweater got too small and had too many holes. I am a person who does not hurry to throw out his clothes—in 2015, I still have a few socks and some shirts from the seventies. But that sweater did disappear somehow. I may have had more Leafs regalia while I was in the air force and at university, but I don't recall. The next fan stuff I wore consisted of a couple of thin T-shirts. While in Montreal I had bought two white tees because I had somehow acquired two iron-on decals, I think they are called. That's how I wound up with a simple Maple Leafs T-shirt and a simple Canadiens T-shirt.

The cotton was pretty thin, as I said, but I wore these shirts to sleep in, to play ball in, and just to look like a hockey fan at the beach in the summer time. They didn't last all that long, but they appeared in quite a few snapshots, and when my daughter was two and a half, one of them showed up in a picture of her. My wife and I had recently bought a giant house in Kerrisdale, and it had so many rooms that little Thea had two—her bedroom and her toys room. Do you remember those big posters we used to have made from family pictures? Somewhere there is a rolled-up poster of Thea standing in her toy room. In the picture she is wearing one of those two T-shirts—I honestly can't remember which, and here is an indication that I am not a fan anymore: I don't really care. I think those T-shirts had shrunk a bit because I had not yet learned that you don't put cotton T-shirts into the dryer. But the one she is wearing in the poster looks like some kind of Great Depression prairie-girl dress made from a flour sack. It hangs right down to her ankles. She doesn't have much hair on her little head.

And a year or two later I got her a cut-rate Calgary Flames T-shirt, may the Lord go easy on me.

Oh, I just remembered—during the early years of the Kosmik League, I often played ball in a faded and tight T-shirt that commemorated my favourite Vancouver Canucks player at the time. This was the remarkable little centre man Bobby Lalonde. He was listed at 5-foot-5, which, everyone agreed, was pushing it. In any case, he was the smallest player in the league. Another piece of clothing I wore to play Kosmic League ball in was my striped engineer's cap that I bought in Osoyoos. It had a couple of buttons on it, my favourite being a reminder of Bobby Wine, a little guy that the brand-new Montreal Expos picked up to play shortstop in the 1968 expansion draft. He hit exactly .200 and got 25 RBIs that season.

You can see the kind of ironic sympathy I exhibited in those days. It's a bit like my cheering for Jerry Korab or my touting Sheldon Kannegeiser on the strength of his name alone. While watching Bobby Lalonde play on TV, or later in the Coliseum, we would cheer, "Bite him in the knee, Bobby!" I loved the feisty little Montrealer. I would never have worn a Bobby Orr T-shirt.

I do have a Toronto Maple Leafs T-shirt. It's almost thick enough to be a sweatshirt. Every once in a while I catch a glimpse of it, seeing the letters TML. What does that stand for, I usually ask myself. Again, I didn't buy it; it was given to me by my sweet ironic stepdaughter Bronwyn. She also gave me my only hockey jersey, a black one with red and white trim, a fan's version of the jersey worn by the Canadian team for the 2010 Olympics. I pulled out a bit of thread so that in the middle of the maple leaf on the chest it now says 01. When it comes to international hockey I favour the Swiss team, and if they don't advance, the Finns.

You know, basketball is my winter sport but I don't buy NBA tank tops. Either you have to wear it with your bare arms or over another shirt. Both look goofy. So in the matter of jerseys that fans can buy, the NHL has it over the NBA. Of course now that we are in the age of saturation marketing, you can get a baseball cap with a logo from any team in any league. I have a prodigious collection of base-ball caps, but only for baseball teams. Well, except for my Chicago Bulls cap, but that was given to me by a member of the 1996 Bulls. If I were a hockey fan rather than a baseball fan, I might collect a few jerseys. I have bought one, but I gave it to my brother Roger, who doesn't know any better than to be a Canadiens fan, and he has it looming over the TV screen in his computer room, red arms extended.

There was that time when only my parsimony stopped me from buying an NHL jersey for myself at Maple Leaf Gardens. This was a time when I was being all ironic in my loyalty—I had a New England Whalers pennant on a wall, an actual New England Whalers puck resting logo-out on a bookshelf, a New England Whalers magne-tized mini-puck on the fridge and a large New England Whalers pin button on my lapel. You'd think that I would be eyeing a New England Whalers jersey that afternoon in

MLG. Nope. I checked them out in a leisurely manner, except for the Philadelphia Flyers jersey, of course, and I came easily to this conclusion: the Quebec Nordiques jersey was the most beautiful, especially the white one with the blue and red trim.

I know how nice a real hockey jersey feels when it hangs so loosely off your shoulders and over your belt. It looks good too, especially on women. One of my favourite moments occurred in Bern, Switzerland, one early evening in November 1965. I was on my way to some indoor café to feed my newly acquired yen for Swiss hot chocolate; there were nice big flakes of snow in the air but the whole scene felt so pleasant and so . . . European, and there they were, two young blonde Swiss misses all decked out in hockey-fan stuff. Toques and scarves and jerseys and some devices to make noise, all in yellow, red and black, the colours of Schlittschuh Club Bern, who would win the second-to-last Europa Cup that year.

Yes, they looked terrific in the lights of Bern's centre. Here's something that looks even better and for which ocular experience you will praise your good luck: a woman wearing nothing but a big hockey jersey.

But this is a hockey book, remember?

You will probably more often have been favoured with the sight of a hefty hip-hop performer wearing an NHL jersey along with a baseball cap with the label still on it, baggy pants, and huge white basketball shoes. That was the fashion around the turn of the century; I don't know what those sports-loving rhyming couplet guys are into now.

It's always interesting to see what sports duds people are wearing in foreign climes. In Europe, where Germans dress up as red Indians and carry bows and arrows around the trim forest, and university students write Ph.D. theses about North American aboriginal authors, the two most popular baseball caps are those pertaining to the Cleveland Indians and the Washington Redskins football team. But New World ice hockey jerseys are not all that ubiquitous. During the summer equinox of 1994, I was trudging around the side streets of downtown Helsinki, while my wife and daughter were either resting or shopping. If I had had my wits about me I would have been looking for a Leonardo painting that was then on loan to some lucky gallery. What I did see was a guy standing on a deserted corner, wearing a Winnipeg Jets jersey. Not so strange: the Jets drafted Teemu Selänne in 1988, but the Finnish Flash played in his home country through 1991. When he joined Winnipeg in 1992, he became that city's favourite athlete and human being. He scored 76 goals in that rookie season, and went on to become the best Finnish player ever. Some people say that he was pretty close to becoming the best player ever. When he retired from the Anaheim Ducks in 2014, he had 684 NHL goals and 1,457 points. I'm wondering whether that guy on the corner of Vironkatu ever got himself an Anaheim jersey.

I've mentioned an even stranger experience in the Yucatán. We spent a few weeks of January 2014 in a grubby little fishing village called Chicxulub, upon which an asteroid fell 66 million years ago, killing all the dinosaurs and Tampa Bay fans on Earth, and on our way there we stayed a week in the beautiful capital city Mérida. While checking out the Mérida Zócalo, which Daphne Marlatt had written a novella about a few decades back, I saw a lot of people in colourful costumes, Mayan and otherwise.

Among the most colourful was a guy I told you about pages ago. We saw him standing with his arms straight out to the sides as if he were about to take flight. He was wearing a cheap yellow baseball cap, tan-coloured pants, a leather shoulder bag and, tucked into his waist, a bright red Montreal Canadiens jersey. On each shoulder and on the back it bore the number 10, and above the 10 on the back, the name LAFLEUR.

Because this guy, perhaps pretending to be that Guy, knew that the Mayans in the Zócalo had no idea what he was wearing, he must lead an active interior life, which is something you can't just assume concerning most NHL *aficionados*. As a Leafs man, I was kind of tempted to bodycheck him against a palm tree, but I am satisfied with my own life of the mind.

NIGHTS *in the* PACIFIC COLISEUM

In 1972, I took the scary plunge. We ended our days as renters and bought a rackly-backly house for $28,000 in upper Kitsilano, between Broadway and 10th. Now I had a wife and baby and two dogs and a house that needed repairs and new appliances, and I had a full-time job in the next city, so my former writing career was now a matter of a few lines every once in a while, written at a window that overlooked one-legged Vietnam vets and Greek immigrants with cans of pink paint.

If you looked out the back window you could see part of the house and yard of the Chittenden family. Little Minda Chittenden was a baby girl the same age as ours, and in fact they would grow up being friends. Her father, Harold, was in a family that had something to do with changing trees into building materials, I think. He was also a Vancouver Canucks fan. One day in late spring of 1972, while the international ice hockey people were planning the big Canada-Soviet showdown, Harold arrived in our kitchen with a proposal: How would I like to go in with him on a pair of season's tickets to the Canucks games at the Pacific Coliseum?

I had never imagined myself as a season's ticket-holder to anything, much less hockey. I don't think I had even contemplated buying season's tickets to the Vancouver Mounties, who played in the Pacific Coast League, a step from Major League Baseball. I mean, how far were the NHL's Vancouver Canucks of 1972–73 from the Major Leagues of anything? Of course, it would be possible to see the storied Boston Bruins and Montreal Canadiens again.

Remember that I didn't have discretionary funds to throw around. I was making hardly any money at my professor job. There was a new house and a pretty new baby, and a partner who had maxed out several credit cards and was looking for new ones. But I had a secret little stash as the result of a couple of literary cheques that arrived on days when I got to the mail first. So, remembering how thrilling it was to stand in the Forum in Montreal, I said yes to sitting in the Coliseum in the east end of Vancouver.

The NHL season was 78 games long that year, so we got tickets to 39 regular season games and two pre-season games. What you did was hold in your hand a thick deck of blue tickets and peel one off for each game. They were pretty good seats, sort of at the blue line in the upper blues. In fact I have a big ticket stub taped into my diary and I am looking at it now. It says Section 24, Row 27 (my favourite number, remember), Seat 13. It says a lot of other things too, including Vancouver versus Boston, and game 35, Tuesday, Feb. 20, 1973, 8 p.m. There is a lot more information on that little rectangle of cardboard, but perhaps one of the most interesting items is this: $5.00. That's right—I got a season's ticket to an NHL stadium for just under $200. I believe that I have heard it rumoured that nowadays you can spend that much to watch one game.

Here was the deal. Sometimes Harold and I would go together. Sometimes he would use both ducats, and sometimes I would take lucky selected friends to see, say, Pittsburgh or Los Angeles. My favourite such occasion occurred on the evening of November 24, 1972. As you know, my father was a Montreal Canadiens fan. It was at least partly because of him that I was a sports fan, and even a hockey fan. But here he was, 65 years old, and he had never seen an NHL game, not even a Vancouver game. I had taken him to see his Cardinals play in his first Major League Baseball game at Jarry Park in Montreal, and that was something, but I was really happy this night in the rink at Hastings Park. This was going to be a bigger deal than the game we'd gone to 17 years before in Penticton.

The Flyin' Frenchmen were really flying that night, the rink was overcrowded with noisy hockey enthusiasts, and there were hundreds of red jerseys to be seen in the stands. I was wishing that the game could have taken four hours to play. I could not imagine what was going on inside that old head that looked quite a lot like my 37-year-old one. Well, expansion baseball and then expansion hockey. Okay. But the Habs won this game 9–1! Jacques Lemaire and Frank Mahovlich made Dunc Wilson's life miserable at the Vancouver end of the ice, and Ken Dryden might have been seen reading a book between Canucks rushes at the other end.

It was Vancouver's third year in the bigs. Two years earlier I had bought a seat for less than face value off a Forum scalper to watch the Canucks in their maiden season. In 1972–73, they were led by Bobby Schmautz with 38 goals and André Boudrias with 40 assists. Dunc Wilson kept his goals-against just a sliver below 4.00. They had a record of 22 wins, 47 losses and nine ties, and finished seventh out of eight in the Eastern Division. The most memorable night of their home campaign occurred against the Philadelphia Flyers, who would finish second in the Western Division.

There was a social experiment starting in Philadelphia. The Flyers had entered the NHL when the league brazenly doubled its size for the 1967–68 season. Playing against organizations such as the Oakland Seals and the Minnesota North Stars, Philadelphia won the Western Division by finishing a whisker below .500. In the next few years their fortunes would fall, and their playoff experience was not satisfactory. But Philadelphia was a big old city in the historic heart of the USA, and they had teams in all the major sports, including at one time two in Major League Baseball. On top of that it had always been a "hockey-crazy" town, and over the course of time its fans would cheer and boo the Arrows, the Ramblers, the Falcons, the Rockets, the Comets, the Phantoms, the Firebirds and so on in various leagues. In 1930–31, the Philadelphia Quakers, led by the great Syd Howe, played a season in the NHL, finishing last in the American Division with a record of 4–36–4. In 1972–73, the city had two "major league" teams, as the World Hockey Association played its first season, and the Miami Screaming Eagles, without ever playing a game in Florida, moved to the City of Brotherly Love and became the Philadelphia Blazers. A year later they became the Vancouver Blazers, and a few years later the Calgary Cowboys before petering out with the rest of the loop.

But the social experiment I was mentioning had little to do with the Blazers. It had to do with the forming of another team, called the Broad Street Bullies. Broad Street, between 13th and 14th, is Philadelphia's main north-south artery, one of the oldest concourses in the USA, running 13 miles through the city and fronting city hall and other historic buildings. The major art galleries are along Broad Street. The ghost of Benjamin Franklin strolls along its sidewalks. Major baseball and hockey buildings are reached by Broad Street, and if some Philadelphia team wins a championship, the parade is held along Broad Street.

In 1972 the Broad Street Bullies were invented and the experiment begun. In Philadelphia they like winners, and they are not afraid of booing their warriors. The Philadelphia Warriors were booed right out of town. On December 15, 1968, at an Eagles game, the fans booed Santa Claus at halftime, and threw hundreds of snowballs at him. Linesmen had been picking things up off the ice at Philly hockey games for years. Remember, the expansion Flyers almost played .500 hockey in their first season, and then, fell below that standard. In their last game in 1972, they missed the last playoff spot on a shot that goalie Doug Favell should have handled, according to spectators.

The Flyers had brought in veteran minor-league coach

Fred Shero to coach them that year, and the newcomer predicted that they would finish second. When they did no such thing he decided that there would be a change in coaching method next year. Shero had invented a system in the minors, but did not apply it in Philadelphia because he figured that major league players (which he had been only briefly) were mature enough to prepare themselves. In the momentous year of 1972–73, things changed. Shero was not a large man but he was tough, and he had his ways. Sometimes he would disappear in the middle of a conversation or interview. Before every game he wrote an inspirational quotation on the dressing-room board. He had his players do weight training all year, something the thin-armed skaters of the Original Six would never dream of. He was also the first leader to hire full-time assistant coaches to work with players on their skills. He had a system, and he had a very fine minor-league record in which his system brought lots of first-place finishes and championships. During his seven years with the Flyers he had a .642 winning percentage.

His system is perhaps best known by the players he coached, and his team is best-remembered for its penalties and brawls. That was the theory for the experiment: could a whole team become thugs and win a majority of their games by slashing, tripping, mugging, highsticking, bashing, biting, punching, kneeing, boarding, butt-ending and so on? Could the Broad Street Bullies stop the Flying Frenchmen and change the game forever? Would the future see large "enforcers" slow down the game and intimidate the little guys who could skate?

In midseason of 1972–73, Philadelphia would hand its

captaincy to their first genuine star, Bobby Clarke, who would get over a hundred points but still contribute to the brutality. You will remember that he had proved his set of values by turning the pre-season tournament against the Soviets into a war, deliberately injuring the opposition's best player. He would get the Hart Trophy after this season, and photographs of him with his wild hair and a wide gap in his mouth ivory thrilled the folks back in Flin Flon, Manitoba. Their Bobby got to complete the trio with Bobby Orr and Bobby Hull.

There have always been hockey fans who liked assault on ice. The only successful movie about ice hockey was about a trio of goonish brothers who would start clubbing opponents when the national anthem played. Later the real brothers who played these fictional siblings would be hired as entertainment by small-time hockey outfits who knew that a lot of their audience didn't think they were a joke. If you are a hockey jersey collector, you can obtain a Hanson brothers one.

So there were a lot of hockey followers who loved the Broad Street Bullies. The NHL was getting to look like TV wrestling—the guys in orange jerseys and long hair would pull into Pittsburgh or Boston, and the fans would scream invectives at them and carry signs describing murderous intent. Once in 1972, the St. Louis Blues were persuaded to climb over the glass in Philadelphia, and swing their sticks at rude fans. Then the Philadelphia police entered the fray and clobbered the hockey players, whose footwear and numbers made for an uneven battle. In the USA, such fracases were popular in minor league hockey, and Fred Shero had seen his share. Now, in all the NHL cities, people were waiting to say "tut-tut" at the Flyers or to throw obnoxious objects at them.

I was in the house four days after Christmas 1972, when the Philadelphia Flyers came to town. I carried no weapon but my razor-sharp wit to use against such big meanies as Dave Schultz, Bob Kelly, Gary Dornhoefer and Don Saleski. It was kind of fun, booing these big orange guys who skated around with their sticks held high. Then the Canucks' Barry Wilcox had the temerity to bodycheck a Flyer into the boards. Saleski showed his displeasure by dropping his gloves and choking Wilcox. If you look at a team picture of the 1972–73 Flyers, you will notice a lot of big facial hair and long locks falling with little finesse behind unhelmeted heads. Well, a fan who had been occupying a pretty expensive seat and probably containing a quantity of beer, decided to rescue Wilcox. He reached over the glass somehow and got a handful of Saleski's soaking wet hair.

The visitors' eyes opened wide. How could they do such a thing to us, a group of talented ice hockey lads? We are the Philadelphia Flyers. We carry hockey sticks into the crowd. Backup goalie Bobby Taylor was the first man up the glass, despite his huge pads and stick. Taylor was said to have some Aboriginal heritage, so, like all such players in the NHL, he was called "Chief" by his teammates. The next player over the glass was fellow-Calgarian Bill "Cowboy" Flett, so in a while, hockey reporters with time on their hands would make numerous jokes about cowboys and Indians. In all, seven Flyers crawled over the glass and started swinging sticks at fans and police, all the while enjoying the fact that they were well-padded except around the head. Several other orange-clad apes kept losing their grip on the glass and falling back to their bench.

I was sitting across the rink, and toward the other end, but I will never forget that curious sight, those padded orange jerseys climbing the glass like large caterpillars with legs. It was a big infestation. I was ashamed of my fellow Vancouverites, and beginning to lose my enthusiasm for the national game. I was glad not to be in the section of the arena where sticks were being swung and beer was being flung. But I had fallen for the trick the Flyers were playing that year—like the villains in the pro-wrestling circuit, they succeeded in arousing performable hatred in the bosoms of paying customers all over the league.

And here's something that interests me—I had to look up the final score in that game. It was 4–4.

Shero's tactics did get the Philadelphia Flyers their first winning season. They finished with 85 points, tied for second in the West with the Minnesota North Stars, whom they beat in the quarter-finals. Then they faced the Montreal Canadiens in the semi-finals, and except for goon fans, people all across Canada were relieved when the Habs easily dispatched the Broad Street Bullies.

But the thug culture was going to change hockey. There had always been guys who fought better than they could skate, but they did not become heroes. U.S. fans in minor-league cities liked lots of fighting because they had not grown up knowing the rules and traditions of the game. In years to come Edmonton's Dave Semenko would become famous as Wayne Gretzky's bodyguard. The toughest Flyer of them all, Dave "The Hammer" Schultz, has a home page on the web. Apparently he is available to give talks about fighting on ice or elsewhere. He once did a refereeing stint with the second-tier wrestling outfit, World Championship Wrestling. Semenko did him one better, having an exhibition bout with Muhammad Ali in 1983.

Well, the Flyers would win the Stanley Cup in 1974 and 1975. How sad. But bad things had been happening for a while. Richard Nixon was re-elected as U.S. president in 1972, the U.S. Air Force was bombing several countries in Southeast Asia, and even when Nixon was forced out of office for being a crook, an ex-football player took over his job.

There was one bittersweet result of the Bullies success in 1972–73. The poor WHA Blazers didn't have a chance in Philadelphia and moved to Vancouver.

WHAT *the* BLAZES?

After that one season, I gave up my Canucks season's ticket. I don't recall why I did, really. Maybe it was the long bus ride to the Pacific Coliseum. Maybe my subconscious was aware of the big drop-off from the Canadiens in an old hockey city in the snow to the Canucks in a logging town in the rain. Maybe I could not join with my neighbouring spectators and the west coast sports reporters in taking grudge matches on ice seriously. Maybe if Wayne Gretzky had arrived earlier than he did, I would have stayed with the NHL; but no, he would have come to town as a rookie in the WHA. So, yes, I would have started going to WHA games.

As it happened, I did.

The sixties and seventies saw big dollars being poured into professional sports in North America, as guys with a lot of new money started swaggering around and buying teams. When there were not enough teams for sale they tried to start new major leagues. Baseball averted the competition by allowing lots of new franchises into Major League Baseball. But in 1960, while baseball was content to call itself "America's National Pastime," a whole new football league started playing and calling itself a major league. The team owners looked at the NFL's draft list and signed three-quarters of the young players on it. By 1966, the NFL said all right, there could be two leagues, and in 1970 all the American Football League teams were embraced.

The flashy American Basketball Association popped up in the 1967–68 season with wild team names, a three-point arc and a red-white-and-blue ball. If you happen to check out the rosters of its hotshot squads, you will spot a lot of basketball Hall of Famers, not because they jumped to the upstart league, but because the Kentucky Colonels and Indianapolis Pacers offered high salaries to young hoopsters. The league slipped from 11 teams to seven, and in 1976 it folded, four of its teams being absorbed into the NBA, along with the three-point arc a couple of years later. One of those teams was the San Antonio Spurs, in recent years the most successful team in the NBA.

Next up was the World Hockey Association. I am sure that you can find books that will fill you in on the whacko owners who started franchises and then shifted them around, often twice a year. Its inaugural season was 1972–73, that year we have been paying so much attention to, and in its seven seasons, there were teams assigned to Edmonton, Calgary (two different teams), Ottawa (two different teams), Toronto, Vancouver, Quebec and Winnipeg.

Also—and this because the league founders wanted greater exposure south the of the border—there were franchises allotted to San Francisco, Phoenix, Philadelphia, Miami, Birmingham, San Diego, New Jersey, New York, New England, Minnesota (twice), Baltimore (which was once in the Canadian Football League, remember), Michigan, Los Angeles, Indianapolis (Racers to go with the Pacers), Houston, Dayton (!), Denver, Cleveland and Cincinnati (Mark Messier's first team).

In the first year, 67 NHLers jumped to the WHA, mainly for bigger salaries or more ice time. The NHL was really pissed off. WHA teams that played in NHL arenas were handed disadvantageous schedules. When the NHL set up the Summit Series they would not let WHAers such as Bobby Hull and Bernie Parent play the Soviets. They were especially pissed off because there were so many really good players in the new league. Think of it: Bobby Hull, Gordie Howe, Frank Mahovlich, Wayne Gretzky, Dave Keon, Bernie Parent, Gerry Cheevers, Derek Sanderson, Mark Messier, J.C. Tremblay, Marc Tardif, etc. etc. On top of that, those crazy WHA owners started inviting European hockey players. The NHL had been content with Stan Mikita, who had been born in Slovakia, eh?

But the most exciting and influential defector had to be Bobby Hull. He was the most feared forward in the league, wasn't he? He was in the habit of scoring 50 goals a year, and his slapshot once penetrated the armour of a U.S. Army Sherman tank. And he was in his early thirties. In mid-1972, he was involved in an interesting conversation.

Unnamed WHA owner: "What's the average salary in the NHL?"

Knowledgeable hockey scribe: "$25,000."

Baseball buttinsky: "$35,000 in Major League Baseball."

Tall black guy: "$43,000 in the NBA."

Bobby Hull: "Heck, I'm making more than that."

Unnamed WHA owner: "Darn it, Bob, you're not your average hockey player."

Bobby Hull: "Chicago's been pretty good to me."

Unnamed WHA owner: "What would it take to get you to slide on over into the new major league?"

Knowledgeable hockey scribe: "Major! Hah!"

Bobby Hull: "Ho ho. I'd sign for a million bucks."

Knowledgeable hockey scribe: "Har de har har."

Unnamed WHA owner, taking out his cheque book: "How about $2.75 million over 10 years, with a million up front?"

Knowledgeable hockey scribe: "Okay, that's major."

When the news came that the Philadelphia Blazers were coming to Vancouver to play on the less favourable dates at Pacific Coliseum, I gave up my Canucks season's ticket and started going to Blazers games. Some things were kind of idiotic or predictive about the WHA experience, and some things were a pleasure. I will mention some of the pleasures (not counting the financial losses taken by owner Jim Pattison). The tickets were a little cheaper, especially because the crowds were so small that you could buy a nosebleed ticket and then sit wherever you found no one else sitting. During pre-game practice I used to get a spot behind one of the goals and nab a puck or two that had been slapped over the glass. The kids that were also there would beg me for the puck, but I would tell them to go get their own. The pucks did not have team logos on them, but they did offer this information: "Made in Czechoslovakia."

Oh, the pleasures. With the smaller crowd you could open up your lungs and make your witticisms heard in the echoing rink. With the choice of seats you could sit in the first row if you settled for being close to one end. One time some Blazer such as Duane Rupp checked Bobby Hull into the boards, and I got a close-up look at the famous hairweave as well as the Golden Jet's nose spread over a significant portion of the glass panel two feet in front of my own face. At the time Bobby Hull was playing left wing on Winnipeg's Hot Line, with Anders Hedberg on right wing and Ulf Nilsson at centre. There is no sense trying to decide what was the best forward line of all time, but I would throw one of my votes to these three Jets. In the 1974–75 season Hedberg got 100 points, Nilsson acquired 120 and Hull amassed 142—this while playing on a team that served half as many penalty minutes as the other squads in the league.

But of course, the Blazers were my team. I tried to get Blaser to come and see them, but he had seen the Summit Series game in the Coliseum. Why would he settle for the Blazers versus the Cleveland Crusaders? The Blazers were not a very good team, but this wasn't Montreal. We were not used to good teams in Vancouver, except in baseball. In that 1972–73 season, the Blazers won 27 games, lost 50 and tied one. The Vancouver Canucks, on the other hand, won 24 games, lost 43 and tied 11. In the following year both teams improved. The Blazers went 37–39–2, while the Canucks went 38–32–10. So, in their two years in Vancouver, the Blazers won two more games than the Canucks did, despite playing four games fewer. And yet it was the WHA team that moved to Calgary for 1975–76. There had been a lot of talk that the Canucks were planning that move, but Jimmy Pattison beat them to it.

So I cheered for the yellow, orange and black team instead of whatever colours the Canucks were sporting. I am green-blue colour-blind, so I would be guessing if I said they were blue and green, but then I suppose that scheme was supposed to represent the forest and the ocean. Yellow and orange and black made for a kind of cheesy combination, I guess you'd say. The NHL is too classy for that: you'd never see the Canucks putting on anything like yellow, orange and black, eh?

Anyway, the Blazers' uniforms didn't look quite right. It was as if some Hollywood costume designer had designed them for a hockey movie in which a lot of the actors would be filmed from the waist up so we could not tell that they couldn't skate. Well, as you know, almost all of the few hockey movies are embarrassing that way.

Unlike the American Basketball Association, the WHA did not bring in any significant rule changes, but the league did introduce some innovations. The most obvious was the noisy pizzazz (which was a little embarrassing in a rink mainly barren of attendees). The PAs played loud rock and roll music before the game and between periods. When the home-team players were introduced the announcer shouted their names over the PA, the house lights were turned off, and spotlights followed Colin Campbell or Danny Lawson as he skated onto the ice, the organ playing loud enough to be heard by drivers on the Second Narrows Bridge. A few years later the staid NBA would pick up on the cheap pyrotechnics and teenagers' music, hip-hop this time, so that I would try to get to a game right after tip-off. As for the NHL? In later years the adolescent music that was blasted at us anytime the puck was not on the ice finally drove me out of the arena. I think that the programmers were afraid that the attendees' attention span would not stretch from play to play without loud drums and guitars to fill the gap.

But the WHA was fun. You kind of felt as if you and the other 3,500 people there were a club, that you knew stuff that other people didn't know. Your face lit up when hot young women skated onto the darkened ice just before faceoff, carrying flaming torches high. You knew that this was stuff the NHL teams would not condescend to do. You had not yet heard of the San Jose Sharks.

But you knew that, really, the WHA was kind of bush. You knew that when you went to their games and picked up the odd souvenir, that you were doing so with irony. And a part of you noticed that if the WHA was doing all the stuff that the NHL was doing, if they were sometimes paying salaries that forced the NHL to up their salaries, and that finally some of these teams in cities that the NHL shunned, such as Edmonton, Winnipeg and Quebec, would be welcomed into the older league, that maybe the NHL was not that far from bush itself. Just saying.

Certainly, trolling through Facebook and other "social media," for information about the Vancouver Blazers is a dispiriting experience. All the entries, including the one on Wikipedia, were composed by people with less than satisfactory familiarity with the English language. Maybe I will have a happier experience if I ever read any books about the WHA.

I think the biggest contribution made by the league was that it made NHL owners wake up to the idea that European players would be fun to watch. Well, unless you were a xenophobic TV commentator.

WHACK 'EM, SMACK 'EM

Not long ago I got to watch my friend Brian Fawcett's daughter Hartlea play ice hockey again. This time it was in a local rink just walking distance from Brian's house in Toronto. Hartlea plays in a few leagues that do not encourage or even allow bashing and smashing, but she and I have a running joke. She always promises to lay a hit on one of her opponents. Hartlea is now a tall defence-person with skating skill, and it must be really tempting for her to deck a forward who comes into her zone with her head down.

Well, whereas the last time I had seen her was from the chilly seats in a posh local arena out in Mississauga, this time Brian and a few other parents and I were standing behind the glass just in back of one of the goal nets. Early in the final period Hartlea nicely lined up another tall girl and rode her gently off the boards and onto the ice. If a bodycheck can be smooth and almost innocent looking, that's what this was. Nobody got hurt. No stickwork was involved, no checking from behind. Back at Brian's place she said she did it for me, and I congratulated her on a job well done.

Okay, I hardly felt guilty at all.

I have no sympathy for those parents who want their little boys' league to allow hits. And when Hartlea lays one on for me, I kind of understand where those parents are coming from. They think of their little sons as extensions of themselves. Pretty soon they will be showing them how to drive their huge pickup trucks.

Like just about everyone else, I guess, I have never liked those All-Star Games that feature no penalties and end with scores of 22–17. On the other hand I quit watching hockey partly because I could no longer sit through games in which the whistle is always blowing to bring the game to a halt while insensitive louts try to disfigure one another. The standard hockey fight, in which the fighters have to hold onto each other because they are wearing skates, is just about the silliest sight in sports. To make it worse, half-drunk fans are spilling beer on the people in front of them while screaming in ecstasy and obscene language. "Kill 'im, Rudy," they yell repeatedly, "Fuck 'im up!" These people remind me of the people standing on the sidewalk below the guy who is threatening to jump off the roof. "Jump! Jump!" they urge. I don't want to be in a building with these people. My friends and I hate it when we are at a Single-A baseball game being played by 19-year-old guys, and some hockey fans get drunk and start their stuff.

I think that the "physical" game is all right. I never minded seeing Bobby Baun or Ed Jovanovski disrupt a hubristic forward. But I have seen the tape of Todd Bertuzzi's murderous attack on Steve Moore, March 8, 2004, more times than I wish to remember. There have been a lot of accusations and counter-accusations and feeble attempts at justification regarding the famous incident and the recent unhappiness shared by the two teams leading up to the most-often viewed incident in hockey history. Colorado forward Steve Moore was not a really good hockey player, but he was not a brute, either. He and his brothers played their college hockey at Harvard University, which is not famous for educating goons. I am not saying that the Ivy League squeezes the stupid violence out of people—George Bush Jr. is said to have gone to Yale. But one look at Todd Bertuzzi and his five-o'clock shadow glower, and you know that you are not in for a seminar on Plato's *Symposium*.

Two and a half weeks before that 2004 game, Steve Moore had laid a tough check on Markus Näslund, Vancouver's best player, and Näslund had left the game, later to be diagnosed with a light concussion and slight injury to an elbow. As a result, the Canucks captain missed three games, no small thing when Vancouver and Colorado were competing for first place in the Pacific Division.

Expecting a power play, the Canucks were nonplussed when veteran referee Dan Marouelli did not call a penalty on Moore. They yelled and screamed on the bench, and they were quoted in the press and on the air as a dissatisfied group. But the League investigated the call made by the 10-year referee, and backed his decision.

So the Canucks went into vigilante mode. If the legal system was going to fail them, they would have to take justice into their own hands, along with their composite sidearms. Vancouver forward Brad May, who had a career made up of suspensions and off-ice arrests, and whose function was clearly not to be a goal-scorer, put out a highly public "bounty" on Moore. Bertuzzi settled for some dirty name-calling.

On March 3, the teams played again, and the NHL made it public that league commissioner Gary Bettman would be at the game in Denver. So would Markus Näslund. Brad May waved his stick and Todd Burtuzzi glowered, but Steve Moore survived the game. Näslund and Bertuzzi had good games; Moore and May were both minus one. The score was 5–5.

Then on March 8, the Avalanche visited Vancouver and clobbered the Canucks 9–2. Not too many people remember the score, nor the fact that Bertuzzi went minus four on the night. Often when a team is getting monumentally embarrassed on the scoreboard, its players go wild in frustration. You see this in basketball, too. But when frustration is added to vigilantism, the outcome can be very ugly. It can make your more civilized spectator ask himself why he is putting out so many dollars to be in such an unpleasant environment.

Ice hockey players have a code. So do certain Sicilian families, street gangs and Old West fictional gunfighters— remember the "Code of the West"? When you hear about these codes, you know that someone is going to "pay the price" for something. The word "honour" is going to get pronounced. "Respect" is going to get mentioned. In the world of the vigilante or *omertà*, there are a lot of serious faces while a lot of silly stuff is being enacted. Hoodlums in expensive suits whispering about "respect" are dangerous but funny. Hockey players with police records putting out bounties on costumed athletes may be making a lot of serious money, but that is just something to laugh about, isn't it? I may be afraid of Todd Bertuzzi, but I can't help smiling when I read about the latest twist in his on-dragging court cases.

The league commissioner was not there for the game on March 8, and Brad May and Todd Bertuzzi knew it. There were enforcers all over the ice, trying to get at Steve Moore. Maybe the Canucks should have put some skill players on the ice—after the first period, the visitors were ahead 5–0. Enforcer Matt Cooke, whose talent was in the area of aggravating enemy players and incurring suspensions, managed to catch up with Moore at the six-minute mark. The whole period was made up of hockey fights, and beer sales were up. At the intermission, NHL executive vice-president Colin Campbell, former scrappy defenceman for the Vancouver Canucks, telephoned the referees and told them to try to keep a lid on the headhunting.

Good luck with that. In the third period Bertuzzi spent all his ice time bumping into Moore, poking at him, daring him to fight. You have seen how schoolyard bullies do this, calling the other guy a sissy, jabbing at him, trying to provoke something to avenge. Moore just skated away. Or tried—now Bertuzzi is grabbing his jersey from behind. Still Moore will not retaliate. This incenses Bertuzzi, who pulls himself closer and slugs Moore in the side of the jaw. You can watch this on the video that I am tired of seeing. Bertuzzi's momentum lands him on Moore's back as Moore is going face-forward to the ice. Bertuzzi grabs Moore's head and smashes his face into the ice. Immediately the warriors from both teams pile on, while the beer drinkers in the seats cheer wildly.

They were slightly less loud 15 minutes later, when Moore was removed on a stretcher. He was taken to Vancouver General Hospital, and later flown to a Denver facility. He had three fractured vertebrae in his neck and damage to the vertebrae ligaments. There was also nerve damage, along with facial cuts and a concussion. Moore has not played an NHL game since, his career ended at five goals and 12 points.

I am not going to go into the complicated legal history of the incident's repercussions. It is a depressing subject. After sitting out for the rest of the 2004 season and being shut out by international hockey during the NHL strike of 2004–05, Bertuzzi played lots more hockey, mainly with Detroit. During all the sordid procedures, he claimed that Vancouver coach Marc Crawford had told the team before that fateful third period that Steve Moore had to "pay the price."

The code, don't you know.

We did not have videos when I was a lad, so if we wanted a taste of mayhem, we had to depend on still photos and written descriptions of events. One of the most famous photos in NHL history shows Maurice Richard shaking hands with Boston goalie Jim Henry after the last game of the 1952 Stanley Cup semi-finals. During the 1951–52 season, opposition players and coaches had been trying everything they could think of to stop or slow down Richard, who was by then clearly the most dangerous offensive threat in the league. Due to injuries, he missed nearly a third of the season's games, and when the playoffs began, the role players, policemen, enforcers and plain goons were sent after the Rocket. Richard was no Gandhi: he knew how to retaliate, legally and otherwise.

By the time of the seventh and deciding game of the semis, Richard's face resembled a butcher's block, but his famous eyes gave the impression that he was possessed. Right from the beginning it was clear that Boston needed to contain Richard if they wanted a shot at the finals, so they hit him hard every time they could catch him. Eventually Leo Labine caught him with a very hard check, and Richard went down. On its way to the ice, his face hit the knee of Boston defenceman Bill Quackenbush, and blood spurted while Richard was knocked unconscious. Bill Quackenbush was not a violent hockey player. He was a great offensive defenceman, who kept on winning the Lady Byng Trophy, not something a defenceman was expected to do. In the 1951–52 season, he gathered a total of six minutes in penalties.

Nevertheless, Rocket Richard was off the ice and into the Forum clinic, where he had a large cut over his left eye stitched and bandaged. He wobbled to the Canadiens bench, where he stayed for a while, trying to remember where he was, hoping that he could focus his panther eyes. He stayed there while the Habs held off Milt Schmidt and the rest of the Bruins. Everyone on and behind the bench knew that Richard was suffering a bad concussion. But it was game 7. The score was 1–1. There were just a few minutes left in regular play. Canadiens coach Dick Irvin sent Richard back onto the ice, asking for greatness.

We know it. Richard somehow got the puck to stay on the blade of his stick while he clawed past the 10 Bruins skaters and flipped the puck at the two Boston goalies. The Canadiens won 2–1, and Roger St-Jean jumped over the boards to take the illustrious photograph of Maurice Richard shaking hands with Jim Henry. Some people have said that it looks as if the Boston goalie is bowing to his nemesis. Maybe he was trying to help Richard stay vertical.

You can see that in 1952, NHL goalie pads were not the king-size mattresses they are today, and that goalies did not wear masks. For this reason you can see that Henry's face took some beating during those playoffs. As to Richard's face: we see the left side only, including a big white bandage above the eye, blood filling the eye socket and ear hole and two streams of blood descending toward the Forum ice.

I think that Canadian fans and journalists saw indomitable spirit, a noble clash of titans, Canadian courage and toughness. I understood all that, and I was nearly sucked in by it. I knew that Leo Labine was a rookie and that Bill Quackenbush was a future Hall of Famer and probably the cleanest defenceman ever to play in major league hockey.

But I was 16 years old, and I was disturbed by this photograph.

There are still a lot of solid hits in hockey, and there are still fights, partly to keep the USAmerican fans interested, but there don't seem to be as many goons around. The Philadelphia Flyers have gone four decades since their goons helped them win their most recent championship, and are now a practically gangsterless team. The attention given to sports concussions in the past few years may have something to do with the change. Over the past 15 years a lot of the heavy stuff has been pushed out of kids' hockey (to the unhappiness of some knuckle-dragging fathers), and maybe that has helped. It's getting to be tough times for the brutish types whose only chance to stay in the show relied on their fists. Too bad about that. We are going to have to play the way the Europeans do.

I tried to do my bit to make hockey fans feel about on-ice hooliganism the way that they, presumably, feel about street mobsters. Shortly after I was made Canada's first Poet Laureate in 2002, I was invited to appear on a pre-breakfast television show on a network called CityTV. On the way to their Vancouver studio, I was shocked by the number of people who were not only up and dressed, but gave the impression that they often do this sort of thing. Of course, I was on the tube to introduce the idea of a Parliamentary Poet Laureate to people who watch television at dawn. I shared the show with Brian Burke, who was then the Vancouver Canucks general manager.

Brian Burke is one of the most intelligent and polite men in hockey, and it was a pleasure to share a studio with him, though I have to say that he looked a lot wider awake than I felt. I shared something else with him: we both got our BAs in history. And we both liked the Sedin twins more than Vancouver hockey fans did—he signed them and I cheered for them. But what was this nice man doing on such an early TV show? It turned out that he liked to cook, and this morning he was going to be cooking breakfast. To do so he took off his well-fitting suit jacket and got to work in white shirtsleeves.

But he was not the only hockey personality in front of the cameras. We were also treated to Fin, the official mascot of the Vancouver Canucks. Fin is a guy dressed up as an orca wearing a Canucks jersey, and in addition to appearing at hockey games, he can be found at any function that involves a charity called Canucks for Kids. He also fancies himself a goalie, and this morning on television he appeared with a street-hockey goal and a big goalie's stick. Along with a Toronto rapster named k-os, I was invited to pick out a hockey stick and face Fin from about four metres. I hefted a left-hand shot Sher-Wood, and gave this killer whale my meanest Chris Simon scowl.

"Okay, Mr. Poet Laureate, see if you can beat Fin!" someone said.

Fast as a jungle cat, I dropped my Sher-Wood to the concrete floor, pulled off my black leather jacket and threw myself at the hapless cetacean, raining (pulled) punches at him. I think that Fin played along, falling into the net and losing his footing. A whole lot of linesmen pulled me off him.

My TV-viewing fans and I agreed that it was great theatre, but I am not sure that Canucks for Kids appreciated the humour—or the comment about hockey fisticuffs.

Certainly, I didn't get the following that seems to have been achieved by a guy in a clown suit who appears on national TV hockey broadcasts. This person's little segment is called *Coach's Corner*, presumably because he was once known as a coach. It's kind of a misleading title, I think: the only coach I know of who works in a corner is a boxing manager, which, I suppose, is kind of apt here, or a professional-wrestling manager, in a show that is more low theatre than sport. The person to whom I refer played hockey for two decades, including one game without personal statistics for the Boston Bruins in the 1954–55 season. Then he coached for 10 years, including six in the NHL. In five years with the Boston Bruins in the 1970s he never had a losing season (the fact that his players included Bobby Orr, Phil Esposito, Johnny Bucyk, Ken Hodge and Gerry Cheevers helped there), and he never won the Stanley Cup.

He came pretty close. In 1977, the Bruins made it to the finals, only to get slapped down in four games by the Montreal Canadiens. In 1978 the Canadiens beat the Bruins in six games. The Boston coach's team was getting closer. In 1979, they faced the Canadiens in the semi-final. During the regular season the Bruins had had a 4–0 record against the three-time defending champions. Now in the semi-finals the scrapping Bruins and the flying Canadiens split the first six games and faced off at the Forum for game 7.

It was the kind of game the TV sponsors love, the visitors going ahead, the home team tying it up, the Forum crowd getting louder and louder in at least two languages. With four minutes left in the third period Rick Middleton put the Bruins ahead 4–3. Then you should have seen kitty trying to bar the door. The only trouble was that there were too many kitties. With 2:22 left in regulation time in a game 7, Boston was called for too many men on the ice. At 1:11, Jacques Lemaire left one of his famous drop passes to the skater behind him, and unfortunately for the guys in black uniforms, that skater was Guy Lafleur. In overtime, Yvon Lambert managed to knock down a pass near the crease and persuade it to cross the line.

The too-many-men-on-the-ice penalty is generally laid at the feet of the head coach, often fairly. In any case, Boston general manager Harry Sinden was not fond of his coach, and took this opportunity to urge different employment on that unlucky individual. The latter coached in Colorado in the following season, and managed to squeeze 19 wins out of the Rockies over an 80-game season. During the season after that, the coach was not coaching anyone.

In the 2001–02 season, he came out of retirement to coach the Mississauga IceDogs in the OHA, getting 11 wins in 68 games out of a feckless squad of juniors. After that he headed straight to his corner.

This is a good old boy from Kingston, Ontario, named Don Cherry. I have been a lifelong fan of the real Don Cherry, who was born in Oklahoma City when I was less than a year old. He grew up in a jazz family and got to listen up close to the best musicians of the forties and fifties. He would become the greatest avant-garde cornet/trumpet player in the second half of the twentieth century. I first heard him in 1958 on Wes Bowen's late-night jazz show on KSL. That's why I scoff when people snort about the Utah Jazz's name. He played with the young Ornette Coleman through the sixties, my favourite decade in jazz. If you need a little help in jazz history, have a listen to Cherry's work on Carla Bley's *Escalator Over the Hill* (JCOA, 1971).

Jazz and hockey in the same book? I have a hunch that most Canadian hockey players don't listen to much classical music or jazz, Wes Bowen's two favourites. They are probably headbangers and hip-hopsters for the main part, though some of them may listen to shit-kicking music. It happens that I have a CD of duets sung and played by Willie Nelson and one Don Cherry. Apparently this one comes from Texas and plays golf when he isn't singing country and western. Okay, I am not that much into country music, but I would rather hear it than *Coach's Corner*.

A few years ago some magazine or radio station did a big survey, asking people to name their favourite "great Canadian." Don Cherry, who spouts right-wing opinions in substandard English, finished high on the resultant list. I am glad that I decided to remain a Canadian rather than to follow my childhood inclination to emigrate southward, but when I hear or see something like that survey, I am in no way "proud" to be a Canadian. Don Cherry comes on as a "staunch Canadian nationalist," but his Canada leaves me out. I am not totally naive, though. I know that more Canadians know who the current "American Idol" is than know who most recently won the Governor-General's Award in fiction. There are organizations that want to keep us unknowledgeable. And I know that hockey's purpose is not to build a Canadian community.

And I am betting that more Canadians buy the video entitled *Don Cherry's Rock'em Sock'em Hockey* than the current GG's Award novel. In fact I know it. The Cherry franchise has produced a new compilation of televised fights and commentary in Cherry's annoying voice every year since 1989, and has sold two million "units." Don Cherry is smart where it doesn't matter whether you're smart. He knows his audience, the good old Canadian boys who don't like gun laws and pantywaist referees. His videos are not called *Pass to'em, Stickcheck'em Hockey.*

Sometimes when Cherry is belligerently dissing some target of his scorn—French-Canadian players, European players, finesse players—he appears to think that most viewers agree with him. He believes in tough players, and supports the "code" I was mentioning a little while back. He scoffed at faceshield-wearers as somehow less than manly. He always disagrees with any NHL rule change that promotes skill over toughness. Often he steps outside the arena of sports, as with his 2015 criticism of northern people for eating seal meat. He does have a lot to say about things to eat: he once referred to Finnish coach Alpo Suhonen as "dog food." You can see the sophistication of his humour along with his manners.

As you might expect of this tough guy, he is all gung-ho about going to war. When Canada did not follow the USAmericans in their first incursion into Iraq (guess how he pronounced that name), he dumped on the government, also finding time to disparage Quebeckers. He went to the U.S., where he had played his hockey, and explained, as the angry unknowledgeable often do, that the CBC is "owned" by the Canadian government and does what it says. Maybe he should have organized a private army and sent them into Iraq armed with hockey sticks. The Bellicose Boppers, they could be called, Rock'em Sock'em Invasion.

Here is what I am pretty sure of: if you make a complaint that this guy in the clown suit with the corrective collar is rude, ignorant, prejudiced, loud, crude and insensitive, he will respond by telling you how rich and popular he is. With his son Tim running the show, he heads in whatever direction the money waves, including that ex-athlete's cliché, the eponymous restaurant. He endorses anything that will feature his photo in the brochure. Not long ago a brochure came with the rest of the "mail" through our innocent mail slot. It extols the health-giving qualities of something called "COLD-FX." It's a fold-out advertisement heavy on pictures and quotation marks. On the front page is a rather rotund Don Cherry in a loud plaid jacket with unmatching tie and head-support shirt collar. He is looking at us with the lack of facial expression one expects of a dangerous bodyguard, and he has one hand on his hip, the other pointed like a handgun at us.

What is "COLD-FX"? The subtitle is "For the prevention and relief of colds and flu." That's right—you can forget about flu shots this year; your bottle of COLD-FX pills says "Trust the science" on it. That's right—12 years of research and seven clinical trials went into providing this miraculous product. Of course, if you look up what is said by doctors who are not in the pay of the product's manufacturers, you read that the product will not prevent colds or flu. A Dr. Jacqueline Shan, Ph.D., D.Sc, is quoted as saying that the product is "a safe and effective natural health product for health maintenance and disease prevention." Dr. Shan is President, Chief Executive Officer and Chief Scientific Officer of CV Technologies, Inc. She is also co-inventor of COLD-FX, Cell-FX and Remember-FX. Phew. If you buy this stuff, it says here, you can "Trust the science," the product having been "CBP certified." Oh, and CBP is owned by CV Technologies.

It goes round and round. Dr. Shan was named Alberta's Woman Entrepreneur of the Year in 2005.

The outfit now operates out of Laval, Quebec. The product is made of American ginseng root. Health Canada has criticized the claims made by the manufacturers. Don Cherry says that he takes it every day. It's kind of a rock'em sock'em medicine.

WELLAND
CANAL DAYS

In an early year of the 21st century, my sweetheart Jean
Baird came to be with me for a while in Vancouver;
then we packed my Volvo with all my goods that were
not in storage, and drove eastward. Our adventures on
the road can be read about in my 2006 book *Baseball
Love*, in which we can be seen enjoying baseball games
and art museums all across the northern United States,
plus a quick visit to Moose Jaw for poetry and amateur
ball. Eventually, we fetched up in Port Colborne, Ontario
(population 18,000), where we would live in what used to
be sin. That funny little town on the Lake Erie end of the
Welland Canal was kind of handy because Jean's big old
house was there, and I was Parliamentary Poet Laureate as
well as University of Western Ontario writer-in-residence.
Soon after we settled there I broke my hip in a dog fight,

so Jean was pressed into a new career as Parliamentary Wheelchair Attendant.

This would be my latest in a series of short residences in the province of Ontario. I had been in the RCAF near Barrie when I was 18, at graduate school in London when I was 31, and a creative writing teacher at Ryerson Institute in Toronto when I was 34. Now I was going to be in Port Colborne for a year, until I persuaded Jean to come and live with me on the left coast. I liked the experience of living in a small town for the first time in years, and getting to know a whole pack of new friends, Jean being a popular person there.

Because of the canal, which enables ships to go from the nose of Lake Superior to the oceans, Port Colborne is a peculiar community. The canal cuts it in half, especially when longliners are headed north and all three bridges are going up. There are two hockey arenas, one on either side of the canal. (Isn't it odd that the building that shelters a big slab of ice is called an arena, given that *arena* means sand in Spanish?) The newer, fancier one is on the east side, and is called Teeder Kennedy Arena.

Teeder Kennedy was born Theodore Samuel Kennedy in Humberstone, a village that would be amalgamated when Port Colborne was amalgamating. Back when I was a radio-listening boy who had never seen an actual hockey game, Kennedy was the guy I decided to be a fan of. Of course I had seen a lot of baseball games, and wouldn't you know it? I was also a fan of Theodore Samuel Williams. He wore number 9. So did Theodore Samuel Kennedy.

Some things you have to leave in childhood, but I still admire Ted Williams because when he was inducted into the Hall of Fame in 1966, he used his induction speech to say that the best Negro League players ought to be there, too. On the other hand, Teeder Kennedy was one of the most prominent holdouts against Ted Lindsay's proposed hockey-players' union.

I never saw the inside of Teeder Kennedy Arena, but we were in Ontario, eh? I was not about to zip up to see the Maple Leafs, but we were in hockey country. So we went one evening to PC's other arena, an old barn that looked as if it had been built a lot earlier than 1962, the official date of construction. Its original name was Port Colborne/Humberstone Arena, but by the time I got there, locals called it West Side Arena. On the outside it had a pretty good paved parking lot, and in the inside it was really really cold, which rinks should be, I suppose. I can imagine that crotchety old-timers preferred it to the new Vale Health & Wellness Centre, "a $32-million, state-of-the-art facility for sport, recreation, health, wellness, entertainment and commerce—all under one roof—the first of its kind in the Niagara region." Along with a lot of other "wellness" stuff, it contains "two NHL-sized ice pads." I'll tell you one thing: because of its name alone, I would not go to see a hockey game there.

For some reason we were a few minutes late for the game. This was unusual, because during our baseball tours we usually get to the park hours ahead of game time to reconnoiter, and again an hour before game time, to be ballpark tourists. But on the evening before the Junior B game at the West Side Arena we got to the edge of the parking lot after the first period started.

"We've missed the first few goals," I said. "This is Junior B here."

"Do you really know something about hockey?" asked this woman who had grown up in snowy Ontario.

By the time we found our cold plank seats, the Sailors were behind 2–1. At the first intermission I got a paper cup of dreadful coffee. I ran a commentary that was worthy of a CBC colour man, and when the third period began with the Sailors down by four goals, I made my second prediction.

"There will be a bench-clearing brawl in the final minute of the game."

Rock'em, sock'em. A bench-clearing brawl in a small cold hockey rink can be really noisy.

The visitors were the Welland Cougars and the score was Cougars 8, Sailors 6. The Sailors were headed for a seventh-place finish, with a record of nine wins, 32 losses, six ties and one overtime loss.

We never did get around to watching another game, partly because I had to drive to London every week, and fly to places like Timmins and Campbell River to deliver Parliamentary poetry from week to week. Yet I am proud to have been a Port Colborne Sailors fan, and I will tell you why: in Port Colborne you can see those big freight ships called lakers anytime that the canal is not frozen tight. Hence sailors are people you will see sailing right through the middle of town all day long.

In fact, the assigning of team names has long been a point of interest to me. The Sailors was a good name in Port Colborne, as the Admirals is a pretty good name for an American Hockey League team in Milwaukee, right there on Lake Michigan. (It would have been neat just to call the team "Hockey," fun to say "the Milwaukee Hockey.") So the Oilers belong to Edmonton. The Hurricanes belong to Hurricane Alley. One of the best names in hockey is the Wheat Kings of Brandon, where they know about such things.

But look what happens when team owners pay attention to someone else's success rather than to the local or specific. A basketball team in Miami takes a run at the faddish naming of teams with a singular noun, and comes up with the Heat, which makes a lot of sense in Florida. Between 2009 and 2014 there was an American Hockey League team called the Abbotsford Heat. I suppose that that cognomen had something to do with the fact that they were the farm team of the Calgary Flames. You see? The Flames were originally based in Atlanta, and their name commemorated the great Civil War burning of Atlanta. Their logo was a capital letter A in flames. When the team moved to Calgary, the A was replaced by a C. My friend George Stanley, an unlikely hockey fan, said that they should have kept the original letter and called the Calgary team the "Flaming A's."

A few valleys east of Abbotsford there is a Junior A team called the Kootenay Ice. I don't think that it's true, but I like to believe that the Abbotsford franchise melted away because the marketing people just didn't pay attention.

Now that I have started, let me carry this rant a little further. The Pittsburgh Penguins were welcomed into the expanded NHL in 1967, and I thought that was all right, because penguins spend a lot of their time standing on the ice. But until the 2010–11 season, the Penguins played in a place called "The Igloo." No matter that the place was officially the Pittsburgh Civic Center—everyone, including the press, called it "The Igloo." I could never figure that one out, as there is nowhere on earth shared by igloos and penguins. Might as well have the San Jose Sharks play in the Tibetan Teahouse. I shudder to think of what the inevitable Las Vegas team will play in.

Now let us return to the Interior of British Columbia. In Kelowna, which is in the North Okanagan Valley, but which bills itself as main city of the Central Okanagan, in the same way that Toronto bills itself as the centre of everything, Kelowna's main tourist industry asset has long been a lake monster called the Ogopogo. Even before I entered this space/time continuum, an image of the Ogopogo appeared everywhere civic and commercial, just as ersatz totem poles could be found everywhere in Vancouver. Usually the monster was Disneyized with a big smile. So the WHL team has a cute hockey-playing lake critter on its jerseys and souvenirs.

And what is the Kelowna team called? The Kelowna Rockets! Now, I am a native of the Okanagan Valley, and I have published a history of British Columbia, but I cannot think of any historical association of Kelowna with rocketry. Houston, no problem. (Actually, to ruin my rant, I have to remind you that they had been the Tacoma Rockets. I don't know or care whether there are rockets or sea monsters in Tacoma.)

Oh, by the way, you can go to a video archive that keeps track of outstanding fights on ice between lake critters and opposing WHL tough guys. The online site refers to "the card." There isn't any pretense at shame—one of the opposing teams is officially named the Hitmen. At least owners and sponsors used to pretend that skating and passing were more important than brawling. I am guessing that some of these people are trying to get fighting recognized as a skill for individual competition at the All-Star break.

It's not just the teams that don't seem to know where they are located. Can you guess the name of the league that embraces these towns: Las Vegas, Boise, Bakersfield and Anchorage? That's right, the East Coast Hockey League. Allen, Texas, is in, along with Windsor, Colorado, and Stockton, California. On a recent baseball trip, Jean Baird and I stayed in a hotel next to the Stockton Ports baseball stadium and the Stockton Thunder's hockey arena. Stockton is a depressed river port, and in 2012 became the largest U.S. city to file for bankruptcy. Most of the downtown is looking old and untended, except for the sports palaces next to the river. The ballpark and the ice rink are grand new edifices.

Oh, and the Stockton Thunder? The logo on their yellow jerseys is a Viking wearing a winged helmet and grasping a hockey stick.

I don't know where they will be in 2015–16. The Calgary Flames have announced that their AHL team will be playing in Stockton. Their name? The Stockton Flames.

So what about the Port Colborne Sailors? I have heard that they are now the Pirates. I guess the owners decided to go for the alliteration.

That Junior B game we went to was not my only hockey experience in Port Colborne. A person felt surrounded by hockey from fall to spring there because southern Ontario people actually drive their cars around with Toronto Maple Leafs flags flapping outside their windows. Even half the old guys riding around on one-speed bicycles are flying Maple Leaf colours. This seemed odd to me, a visitor from the edge of the world. I remember a similar feeling when I went to the University of Western Ontario in 1966. When I was still an undergraduate at University of British Columbia, I worked Saturday mornings in the library and then amused myself by going to UBC football home games after work. There would be about a hundred of us, carrying mickeys of some cheap hooch and stupidly imploring the female cheerleaders to perform cartwheels. But at UWO they had a big pep rally the night before a home game, attended by young women in fur coats and guys in cable-knit sweaters. On game day the football stands were full, there was a band playing and students attended wearing Mustangs' colours. They shouted the Western fight song without irony. I felt as if I were in a USAmerican movie.

My most exciting hockey experience in Port Colborne? Going to see the neighbours. Jean and I lived in a big house with a big corner yard on Fielden Avenue, and in the first house on the next block lived John Horvath. Horvath had recently stopped running the Tastee-Freeze soft ice cream place, an A-frame that, when I first saw it, was closed for business, but sported a poster welcoming me to Port Colborne for George Bowering Day, which had more to do with poetry than with hockey. I wasn't interested in that so much as I was in the name Horvath.

You remember Bronco Horvath, don't you? Back in the days when hockey teams sported forward lines with snazzy nicknames, Bronco Horvath had been a member of the Uke Line for the Boston Bruins, the successors to that team's famed Kraut Line. The Kraut Line was great; it consisted of Woody Dumart, Bobby Bauer and the immortal Milt Schmidt. They'd all grown up in the pretty darned German Kitchener, Ontario. In 1939–40, they finished first, second and third in league scoring. In 1942, they all joined the RCAF to fight the Krauts.

As soon as the Kraut Line ceased operation, along to the Bruins came the Uke Line. They were pretty darned good. One year each of them scored over 20 goals, and that had not happened before. Johnny Bucyk and Vic Stasiuk were from Ukrainian communities in Alberta, and Bronco Horvath grew up in Port Colborne, Ontario. He has a Hungarian name because his family's home town was in Hungary before it was ceded to Ukraine when the Hapsburg Empire was broken up after the First World War.

Bronco played for five other NHL teams, but he is remembered most for his Uke Line days as a Bruin. In the 1959–60 season, he tied Bobby Hull for the league lead in goals scored (39) and lost the Art Ross Trophy to Hull by a single assist. He played six years in minor professional hockey before making the NHL, and dipped back into the American Hockey League from time to time, finishing his career with the Rochester Americans in 1969, just under the age of 40. He played more games in the AHL than in the NHL, and indeed was elected to the AHL Hall of Fame.

His brother John, two years his junior, never quite skated in an NHL game, having been born just a little too early to be around for expansion. He started his minor pro career with the Portland Eagles and played most of his career with the Johnstown Jets before ending up with Toledo of the International Hockey League. When Bronco's playing and coaching days were over, he retired to Cape Cod, where he had coached the Cape Cod Cubs of the Eastern Hockey League. His brother John retired to Port Colborne, where I was lucky enough to meet him in 2003.

My friend Brian Fawcett was visiting us and taking part in some literary festival tomfoolery we were enjoying. He grew up as I did, enjoying the sport while never playing it. When he heard that John Horvath was virtually our next door neighbour, his eyes lit up behind his round glasses. Jean made a date, and next day she marched us across Elgin Street for a visit. This was small-town Ontario, so we got tea and coffee and cookies and cake: good old-fashioned Canadian hospitality. We endured the cheery introductory talk with John and Beryl, but Brian and I were itching to get downstairs, where the good stuff was.

The entire downstairs was an ex-athlete's den. There were comfortable chairs to sit in and sling the bull for hours. Lots of statuettes and silver-chrome cups on shelves and tables, framed photographs all over the walls, glossy prints and clipped newspapers. Quite a few of the pictures featured Beryl (Laing) Horvath in a bathing suit, and it was not just out of politeness that Brian and I spent some time looking at them. Beryl won more beauty contests than John won scoring races. But most of the space was a hockey den, and that is what Brian and I were all excited about. We found a way to turn on the tap, and John Horvath's stories came pouring out.

I once met 96-year-old Connie Marrero, the one-time Washington Senators pitcher, in his son's Havana apartment, where he recounted the pitch selection he used to strike out Ted Williams; he specified the date and the ballpark and the weather and the inning and the number of outs and baserunners. A lot of ex-athletes are like that. So I just had to mention Rocket Richard, and John told us about November 20, 1951, at Cambria County War Memorial Arena in Johnstown, Pennsylvania.

The Johnstown Jets of the EHL had a deal of some sort with the Montreal Canadiens, and some of their players had signed contracts with the Habs. I don't think that the 21-year-old Horvath was one of those, but another 21-year-old, Don Hall, was the Jets' most popular player, and had signed a C-form with Montreal. On November 20, the Canadiens were in town for an exhibition game, and the young Jets were both star-struck and eager to show their wares.

A total of 1,638 fans came out to see the 30-year-old Rocket, who had scored 42 goals in 65 games the year before, and to see how the young Jets would do against the Stanley Cup finalists. The Jets players had been told to skate with the Rocket but not to rough him up. Richard scored six goals that night, and the Canadiens won 10–2. The Jets goals were scored by Buster Barber and John Horvath. In his basement museum, John remembered where he had put the puck 52 years earlier. Now, 12 years later I don't remember.

For the first quarter of his last season, 1955–56, John was up with the Cleveland Barons, where he got to play with Ike Hildebrand, one of the most famous minor league players of the forties and fifties. Hildebrand was 5-foot-7, and 145 pounds, a Ted Lindsay–type, who scored 91 points for Kansas City in the USHL in 1950–51. Over his career he played 41 games in the NHL, and would suit up for Belleville's senior hockey McFarlands in his forties. John Horvath liked that speedy little Winnipegger, but he would never emulate Ike in middle age. Instead he and Beryl would preside at Horvath's A-Frame drive-in in their home town.

John was just over 25 years old when he hung up his skates and pulled off his Toledo Mercurys jersey for the last time. I was a brat in the RCAF at the time. But I didn't feel like a kid in that basement at Fielden and Elgin. There we were, looking at memories of a world I had only imagined in my own room in the basement of *my* home town.

HELLO,
CANADA...

You will remember that often before heading down to my desert basement in Oliver I would spend a couple hours in Maple Leaf Gardens. That's where I learned the necessity of the imagination while listening to Foster Hewitt with his funny Ontario accent (the prime minister sounded like that, too) tell me about a game I had never seen being played in a place I had never been. Yes, the necessity of the imagination, but also its limits. As I've told you, when Foster said that he was broadcasting from high in his Venetian boat I had no idea what that looked like—maybe, I figured, he was wearing a horizontally striped shirt. As to the question of "gardens"? I figured that must be some peculiar Eastern Canadian usage I would understand once I got to Toronto sometime in adulthood.

I did get to the centre of the universe eventually, getting to Maple Leaf Gardens twice. The second time was to almost buy that Quebec Nordiques jersey that till this day I wish I had. The first time, though, I was in the company of some poets who managed to buy four tickets to a game against the Detroit Red Wings. In the early spring of 1970 such a purchase was not an overly difficult thing—the Maple Leafs were on their way to a last-place finish in the East Division. They finished 21 points behind fifth-place Montreal, and were the only team in the division to have more losses than wins.

So my old friend the poet David McFadden (with whom I would later go to preposterous Blue Jays games at Exhibition Stadium), the playwright David Young, and someone else (probably a novelist named David) got seats up fairly high between the blue line and the corner, and watched the Detroit Red Wings lay a hurt on the locals.

Of course, I was sitting there saying inside my head, "Hey, I am in Maple Leaf Gardens. There doesn't seem to be a gondola. Jeepers, Maple Leaf actual Gardens." By then I had been to a number of games at the Montreal Forum, but this was Foster Hewitt's house. I had learned that Danny Gallivan had it all over Foster Hewitt. I loved the way Gallivan made the language soar, no matter how corny, the way he always said "Big Frank Mahovlich," while Foster Hewitt could not learn how to say "Cournoyer." Every time he made it rhyme with "employer," viewers and listeners would shout in unison: "Corn! Why! Eh!"

So I was really glad to be there. People had not started talking about a "bucket list" yet, but I knew that I had taken another step to the big goodbye/hello. Though I am now officially a geezer, I still hope that I can make it to baseball games in all the Major League parks, but I don't think I ever did have an ambition to get inside all the NHL arenas.

It was interesting but it did not feel like a dream, much less a dream come true. I didn't see the ghosts of Busher Jackson, Ace Bailey, Syl Apps and Turk Broda. There was no otherwordly glow anywhere. One was aware of concrete more than history. When I looked upward, I saw a square ceiling with all kinds of equipment and stuff dangling from it. It looked more like a factory than a sports cathedral.

And the Red Wings thumped the Maple Leafs good.

There is something you should know about David McFadden. He has never wanted to seem the everyday journalist, poet, sports fan or person. I had only sort of noticed that he had been carrying an attaché case when we arrived on Carlton Street. I forgot all about it during the game. I suppose that Dave had shoved it under his seat. He and David Young and I had talked manically all through the game, though I don't know whether the fourth guy said anything. At the end, when the announcer gave us the game's three stars, in the wrong order as is common in hockey, I saw McFadden snapping open his attaché case, revealing its contents—books by David McFadden. We were in the way of some impatient Leafs supporters who were trying to join the crowd surging toward the exits.

"Wait," hollered McFadden, trying with little success to be heard above the grumbling thousands, "I am prepared to read my work aloud. If commanded to, I will sell you some poetry."

We other three surrounded him closely, in order to protect him from the masses, or vice versa. Eventually we were on the street, asking each other where we were going. Somehow, in the human traffic jam along Carlton and Yonge, we lost David Young. The rest of us stumbled down the subway steps, listening to McFadden extol his new favourite bar with unusually intelligent barmaids in it. I can't remember whether I bought a poetry book off him.

David McFadden has published a lot of poems and I have read them all, and I have written several essays about them, but at this moment I do not remember any McFadden poems about hockey. I do remember one of his short stories in which his fictional counterpart Brownie is going door to door one November night in Hamilton trying to straighten up some Christmas card orders he had not delivered yet. Everybody who comes to the door is watching the Montreal hockey game because the Leafs are on the west coast. Hockey night in prose.

In fact, even though newspapers such as the *Vancouver Sun* will devote 80 percent of their sports section to ice hockey on August 1, poets and other writers tend to look elsewhere. More than any other sport, baseball has provided inspiration for poems and fiction in North America. Boxing is probably in second place, but by quite a margin. There is some hockey poetry and fiction, of course.

One of our most interesting hockey poems is an early one by the remarkable Al Purdy, a kind of anti-Cherry piece called "Hockey Players." Purdy is by no means an enemy of hockey. He was brought up in small-town Ontario, after all. He sat in cold rinks and wondered whether his car would start after the game. He calls it "a game played for passionate stockbrokers," but he frames a forward's rush in religious terms such as "resurrection" and "crucifixion," though it is watched by "television agnostics." Yes, this is no innocent patriot blindly devoted to a team or game. But on the other hand, he honestly and metaphorically admits to the sudden excitement of a three-man rush:

> We sit up there in the blues
> bored and sleepy and suddenly three men
> break down the ice in roaring feverish speed and
> we stand up in our seats with such a rapid pouring
> of delight exploding out of self to join them why
> theirs and our orgasm is the rocket stipend
> for skating thru the smoky end boards out
> of sight . . .

Then he switches focus, and comes up with the liberal's inescapable paradox, or maybe ethical conflict:

> And how do the players feel about it
> this combination of ballet and murder?

It is the conflict felt by thousands of intelligent and sensitive followers of the game. We are used to seeing semiliterate young men who crash and slash because "it's my job, it's my way to stay in the game." For a long time the NHL has been dreamed of as an escape, a refuge for undereducated and caste-formed youths who yearn for a life that is not defined by unemployment or a dead-end job. Yet once in a while we see someone like Ken Dryden,

who went to an Ivy League university, then played spectac-
ularly for the Montreal Canadiens, became a lawyer and
author and Parliamentarian. He could have gone straight
from campus to courtroom, but there was something in
him that was hockey to Al Purdy's poetry. Purdy did not
have Dryden in mind, this goalie with a poet's name when
he wrote:

> And what's the essence of a game like this
> which takes a ten-year fragment of a man's life
> replaced with love that lodges in his brain
>   and substitutes for reason?

I like the way this poem swings back and forth
between lovely excitement and unremitting realism. The
hockey player who earlier in the poem created the income
for stockbrokers later ponders on

> your aching body stretched on the rubbing table
> thinking of money in owners' pockets that might be
>   yours
> the butt-slapping camaraderie and the self-
>   indulgence
> of allowing yourself to be a hero and knowing
> everything ends in a pot-belly

The last two stanzas present the dualism the poem has
been suggesting, perhaps with the pathos that is such a
strong challenge against the simple rah-rah enthusiasm
sought by the advertising world. The penultimate stanza
starts by continuing the scenario of the heroic skaters

flying over the world, then ends with this rather over-simple couplet:

sing the song of winning all together
sing the song of money all together

—and then the last stanza quickly presents an image the contrary of both winning and money:

                        (and out in the suburbs
there's the six-year-old kid
whose reflexes were all wrong
who always fell down and hurt himself and cried
and never learned to skate
                        with his friends)

Purdy's poem includes a number of bad patches and inaccuracies (you don't stand in your seat; your aching body leaves thinking to your mind), but it has some of the finest lines about Canadian hockey, my favourite being his description of the game as "this combination of ballet and murder."

Even I once wrote that crummy poem about hockey, when I was young and still following the NHL, but I don't do it anymore. I don't know whether young writers are still writing hockey poems or hockey stories, but I think a lot of them are still watching games on television. Even in Toronto, while making jokes about the feckless Leafs, who fill the Air Canada Centre for every game, writers like to watch their team even while the Leafs lose to Tampa Bay.

It so happened that I was invited to speak to a creative writing class at UBC during the early summer of 2011. In the late spring the Vancouver Canucks had gone to the Stanley Cup finals against the Boston Bruins. It was Vancouver's third trip to the finals, and they had lost the two previous series to U.S. east coast cities, the Islanders sweeping them in 1984, and the Rangers beating them in seven games in 1994. After that game the Vancouver fans showed their love of professional hockey by performing a fiery riot in downtown Vancouver. Now in the 2011 finals the Bruins came through, winning the last two games, and encouraging the Vancouver fans to burn and smash downtown Vancouver again.

It so happened that when I spoke to that creative writing class I started by taking stuff out of my book bag—books, manuscripts, notebooks—and a nice big fuzzy Christmas stocking, which I hung by the blackboard with care. I do not remember how I had come into possession of this Christmas stocking some years earlier, or to whom I have given it since, but I can describe it. In colour it was black and yellow with white trim. Knitted on both sides was a nice big letter *B* in the middle of a spoked wheel. The aspiring young writers in the classroom looked as if they wanted to start a riot, but I think that they were employing the irony these youngsters are noted for.

That Bruins sock joined almost all of my hockey souvenirs when I departed my big Kerrisdale house. A couple of years ago a stranger came around and bought the *Blueline* and *Hockey Pictorial* magazines that had been moving with me back and forth across the country since I bought them in the fifties. I used to have my Montreal hockey stick in a metal Toronto Maple Leafs canister along with a baseball bat, a tennis racquet and a putter, but I sawed down my hockey stick and retaped it for my daughter. The canister disappeared along with a lot of other things when I moved house around the turn of the century. My WHA pucks went the same way, I guess, and all my Hartford Whalers stuff—puck, pennant, fridge magnet and ball cap.

While this was happening, hockey filled less and less space in my life. As I got more and more channels on my TV, and as *Hockey Night in Canada* became just about any night, I couldn't be bothered watching the Canucks play the Blue Jackets. I have a friend who every year used to buy three season's tickets in the nosebleed tier at General Motors Place; he and his daughter usually used two of the tickets and gave the third to a guest. I was the guest a few times, and I remember that the old thrill of the hockey rink almost made it out of my deep memory. But there was too much on the minus side to bring me back to the ice arena. The seats one gets to rent for a couple of hours now cost 25 times what my seats at the Pacific Coliseum had set me back. Now lights were flashing and some shill was hollering on the PA before the game, and as you know whenever the game clock wasn't running, we were assailed by over-loud teenagers' head-banging music.

So I told my friend Jim that I would not be insulted if the extra ticket went to someone else. A year or so later Jim said to hell with live hockey, too.

But people are still paying big bucks and going to hockey games, even when the Edmonton Oilers play a game at

Jobing.com Arena (now renamed Gila River Arena) in Glendale. I think there are a lot of rich, bored, nonreading Canadians spending the winters in Phoenix. Last spring Jean and I were in Dallas to see a Major League Baseball game played somewhere about an hour's drive from downtown. When we made it back to downtown Dallas we went to a quiet bar we had found and ordered our Friday night manhattans, specifying rye instead of bourbon, and while we were sipping and relaxing after the sight of some Mexican-American lads ostentatiously saluting George Bush, who was on the Jumbotron, our peace was, as they say, shattered by a bunch of drunken louts in green jerseys. These oafs had apparently seen the Dallas Stars win or lose several hours ago, and wanted everyone to know it.

Hockey in Texas. Here we were on a baseball tour through a state in which we saw teenagers carrying assault rifles along city streets, and we kept being reminded that the place was full of hockey fans. And these Texans were not carrying petitions aimed at reducing the gratuitous violence in the game. I did find one delight in the Lone Star State, that being the chicken-fried dill pickles at a seaside chain eatery in Corpus Christi, but on the way there we stopped for gas at a desolate crossroads north of the smokestack forest. I went inside the little shed to pay, and there I saw a 350-pound guy in a Dallas Stars jersey, sitting and watching a hockey game on his bleary little television set. I think Florida was playing Buffalo.

We went further south this winter again, to our fishing village non-resort at the south end of Jalisco state. We rented a house situated between the ocean and the main street of the village. Right across Avenida María Asunción was a gringo bar called Jalapa Joe's, into which I have seldom gone; but one evening I rewarded myself for getting four pages done that day, and went across the street and sat at the bar. I was not the only Canadian in the joint; in fact most of us were Canadians. While sipping my restorative beverage, I was half-turned to my left in order to watch a television on which the Toronto Raptors were losing a game to the Memphis Grizzlies. I had to look past a guy who was seated to my left, looking to his right past me to watch the Toronto Maple Leafs losing to the Ottawa Senators. Right there, I knew, was a scene that characterized my life as a sports fan.

YOU CAN'T
SKATE HOME AGAIN

When I was a schoolboy in the South Okanagan, it was my ambition to become a professional sportswriter for a big city newspaper. I had some sportswriting heroes, such as Shirley Povich and Grantland Rice, but when I got older I gave up my ambition because I figured I couldn't come up to this standard of observation: "Dale McCourt scored four goals Thursday night as St. Catharines Fincups, representing Canada in the World Junior Hockey Championships, thrashed Poland 14–0 behind goalie Al Jensen's 26-save shutout."

I would have leapt to the conclusion that the Fincup players spent most of their time farther up the ice.

For a while I entertained the notion of being a television sports commentator, but then I once heard one of those experts say during an intermission that "the Canucks would like nothing better than to tie this game up in the second period."

Maybe, I thought, I should go into poetry or fiction instead of this hockey reportage I don't understand.

I have done some sportswriting from time to time. Recently I came across some cuttings of stuff I published in the *Oliver Chronicle* when I was a sprat, and I had to agree with myself that the writing was a lot better than the hockey reportage I have read in that paper lately. I suspect that that reportage is now done by someone who is not a writer so much as a person connected with OMAHA. No, not the biggest city in Nebraska, but rather the Okanagan Mainline Amateur Hockey Association.

Such organizations sprang up all over the province after the Vancouver Canucks made it to the big time. Boys (and sometimes girls) wearing hundreds of dollars' worth of gear and costumes are skating in every region from the frozen north to the semi-arid south to the rainswept islands. Everything is organized. If you thought that Little League (etc.) grown-ups were well organized in their ambition to take the structure away from the kids on the sandlots and give it to the committees and the sponsors, you ought to see the grown-ups in "minor" hockey. According to the young skaters' ages, they will be Novices, Atoms, Peewees, Bantams, Midgets (yes, still), Juveniles and eventually Juniors. Oh, and in case you were wondering who this is all about, some communities have a pre-novice division called Timbits.

So, remember that frozen pond up in the hills west of my hometown, Oliver? I would like to think that there are still kids hiking up there with skates hanging around their necks and snow shovels and hockey sticks over their shoulders. But I am not going to go up there and look. Nowadays, just as in Ontario and Saskatchewan, every little town has its ice rink. That's where the 100 Mile House Wranglers hang out. Or the Beaver Valley Nitehawks. Early in the calendar year there will be minor hockey tournaments in Sicamous and Rutland, and a lot of parents getting up and driving their SUVs in the dark.

So where I grew up seeing only basketball and baseball there is now South Okanagan Minor Hockey. Baseball made my Valley childhood a dream, but then along came television, and Sundays were devastated. There were no more adults playing ball. The loveliness of having a league with league standings was now replaced by commercials and electronic signals that told us that we were now nowhere, that baseball happened on Saturday in Chicago.

And television brought with it hockey. The heavenly game would be replaced by the brutal Ontario-Saskatchewan game. Parents would prove that they were Canadian by getting up in the dark and driving to a cold building to stand in heavy coats, clutching Styrofoam cups of over-cooked coffee. Most of the action would happen in Osoyoos, at a place called the Sun Dome Arena. Now, when I hear the word "dome" I think of Florence or Washington or Jerusalem. Yes, there is a lot of sun in Osoyoos, but I have not seen a dome in the whole region, except for the place where the Sikh orchardists worship. As for arena, well yes, it is the word for sand in Mexico, and there is quite a bit of that commodity in the Okanagan Valley. And I suppose that Calgary has demonstrated that a dome doesn't have to be dome-shaped.

But I will give the Osoyoos outfit marks for the name of their Junior B team—the Coyotes. When I was growing up in the bottom part of our valley, the coyote was my favourite animal. Kids I knew spent a lot of time trying to imitate coyotes. My pal Bill and I called ourselves The Coyote Kids, and had a secret code done in coyote howls. Sometimes on my solitary ramble in the hills I would come across a solitary coyote and start this game with him: I would run after him and he would wait till I got fairly close, and then tear off and sit down at a distance, tongue hanging, while I caught my breath and ran after him again, and so on.

So I give them a point for the name. Unfortunately, the logo on their chests was plagiarized from one of the jerseys of the Arizona Coyotes. These Junior B dawgs, at least at the time of writing, vie against the Summerland Steam, the Kelowna Chiefs, the Princeton Posse and the North Okanagan Knights in the Okanagan Division of the Okanagan/Shuswap Conference of the Kootenay International Junior Hockey League. So it goes in the province.

Some minor hockey games are played in the Oliver Arena, which is in a big recreational area where the Oliver Elks used to play baseball games against Trail and Kamloops. I think the arena started as a curling rink, where my father and mother picked up yet another sport in later life. Actually, the Oliver Arena is just around the corner from Heritage House, where my mother now lives, and just down the street from the South Okanagan General Hospital, which my father's committee worked so hard to get established. I wonder whether hockey players play with abandon when they know that there is an emergency ward a few hundred metres away.

Yes, things have really changed in my home town, I was thinking the last time I went to visit my mother. But they had changed a lot more than I knew: there is a branch of the Okanagan Hockey School in a nice town named St. Pölten in Austria. Don't ask.

Anyway, I wonder whether I would have had the nerve, and whether my family would have been able to scare up the money for me, to go out for hockey with Mickey and Billy and Frankie and Ron and Freddy. Nowadays the players' names are Tyler and Colby and Kyton and Bailey and Brandon. My kid brother's daughter has a son who worked his way up from novice in Osoyoos, and he has one of those funny new names.

Unlike my classmates who hiked up past Fairview Road to play their referee-less games in the middle of the twentieth century, Okanagan boys and girls now play with no snow on their little faces. They do their beautiful skating indoors, where their sleep-deprived parents can have Timbits with that awful coffee.